MICROSOFT OFFICE
EXCEL 2003
QuickSteps

JOHN CRONAN

McGraw-Hill/Osborne

New York Chicago San Francisco
Lisbon London Madrid Mexico City
Milan New Delhi San Juan
Seoul Singapore Sydney Toronto

McGraw-Hill/Osborne
2100 Powell Street, 10th Floor
Emeryville, California 94608
U.S.A.

To arrange bulk purchase discounts for sales promotions, premiums, or fund-raisers, please contact **McGraw-Hill**/Osborne at the above address. For information on translations or book distributors outside the U.S.A., please see the International Contact Information page immediately following the index of this book.

This book was composed with Adobe® InDesign®

MICROSOFT® OFFICE EXCEL 2003 QUICKSTEPS

890 WCK WCK 01987

ISBN 0-07-223228-5

PUBLISHER / Brandon A. Nordin

VICE PRESIDENT AND ASSOCIATE PUBLISHER / Scott Rogers

ACQUISITIONS EDITOR / Roger Stewart

ACQUISITIONS COORDINATOR / Jessica Wilson

TECHNICAL EDITOR / Marty Matthews

COPY EDITORS / Chara Curtis, Harriet O'Neal

PROOFREADERS / Chara Curtis, Kellen Diamanti, Harriet O'Neal

INDEXER / Kellen Diamanti

LAYOUT ARTISTS / Bailey Cunningham, Keith Eyer

ILLUSTRATORS / Kathleen Edwards, Pattie Lee

SERIES DESIGN / Bailey Cunningham

COVER DESIGN / Pattie Lee

To Marty Matthews

… author, mentor, and friend extraordinaire, who brought me into this computer-related writing world over a dozen years ago (not fully sure whether to curse you or thank you for that!)

About the Author

John Cronan was introduced to computers when he was in college, over 25 years ago. Since then, he has maintained a keen interest in and utilization of their ever evolving features. John first became involved in writing and editing computer-related materials over 12 years ago. In the ensuing years, he has worked on dozens of books and software product manuals, additionally performing technical reviews of other authors' works in the course of operating his own technical writing and editing business. *Microsoft Office Excel 2003 QuickSteps* is John's first work as sole author. Recent books published by **McGraw-Hill/** Osborne that John has had a hand in creating include *Windows Server 2003: A Beginner's Guide, FrontPage 2003: The Complete Reference* (Matthews), and *Introduction to Windows 2003 Server* (Ecklund).

John and his wife Faye (and cat, Little Buddy) live in historic Everett, WA.

Contents at a Glance

Contents

1

2

Acknowledgments

It might not take a village to publish a book but it certainly takes a dedicated, professional, and forgiving team–especially for a first timer! Thanks to one and all!

Marty Matthews, technical editor, went well beyond the task at hand, as always, and provided immeasurable support as QuickSteps series project manager, you-name-it editor, and basic sounding board. Couldn't have—wouldn't have—done it without you Marty.

Chara Curtis and **Harriet O'Neal**, copy editors, somehow took words written by a guy who got C's in English and turned them into readable (and grammatically correct) text, and doing so with timely comic relief.

Bailey Cunningham, series designer and layout artist, and **Keith Eyer**, layout artist, through their talent of fitting round pegs into square holes were able to produce, under severe time constraints, eye catching and well-organized pages from a complex format.

Kellen Diamanti, indexer/proofreader, for finding things that wouldn't be seen by an electron microscope.

Carole Matthews, fellow QuickSteps series author and all around great person, thanks for being there and listening when I needed someone to commiserate with.

Faye Sturtevant, wife and best friend, thanks for just being you.

Introduction

QuickSteps books are recipe books for computer users. They answer the question "How do I...?" by providing quick sets of steps to accomplish the most common tasks in a particular program. The sets of steps are the central focus of the book. *QuickSteps* sidebars show you how to quickly do many small functions or tasks that support primary funcitons. Notes, Tips, and Cautions augment the steps, yet they are presented in such a manner as to not interrupt the flow of the steps. The brief introductions are minimal rather than narrative, and numerous illustrations and figures, many with callouts, support the steps.

QuickSteps books are organized by function and the tasks needed to perform that function. Each function is a chapter. Each task, or "How To," contains the steps needed for accomplishing the function along with relevant Notes, Tips, Cautions, and screenshots. Tasks will be easy to find through:

- The Table of Contents, which lists the functional areas (chapters) and tasks in the order they are presented

- A How-To list of tasks on the opening page of each chapter

- The index with its alphabetical list of terms used in describing the functions and tasks

- Color-coded tabs for each chapter or functional area with an index to the tabs just before the Table of Contents

Conventions Used in this Book

Microsoft Office Excel 2003 QuickSteps uses several conventions designed to make the book easier for you to follow. Among these are:

- A ⚙ in the Table of Contents or the How To list in each chapter references a QuickSteps sidebar in a chapter.

- **Bold type** is used for words on the screen that you are to do something with, such as click **Save as** or open **File**.

- *Italic type* is used for a word or phrase that is being defined or otherwise deserves special emphasis.

- <u>Underlined type</u> is used for text that you are to type from the keyboard

- SMALL CAPITAL LETTERS are used for keys on the keyboard such as ENTER and SHIFT.

- When you are expected to enter a command, you are told to press the key(s). If you are to enter text or numbers, you are told to type them.

- When you are to open a menu, such as the Start menu or the File menu, you are told to "open **Start**" or "open **File**."

How to...

Chapter 1

Stepping into Excel

This chapter explains how to open Excel, interpret its screen and toolbars, and then set them up to meet your own needs. You will learn how to get Help, online or offline or by doing research over the Internet. You will see how to use the Office Assistant. This chapter will also show you how to end an Excel session.

Start Excel

Excel can be started by several methods. Your choice of method depends on convenience, personal style, and whether you are opening a new or existing workbook. After Excel is opened, several features are available to you to personalize the way you work.

Use the Start Menu to Load Excel

Normally, the surest way to start Excel is to use the Start menu.

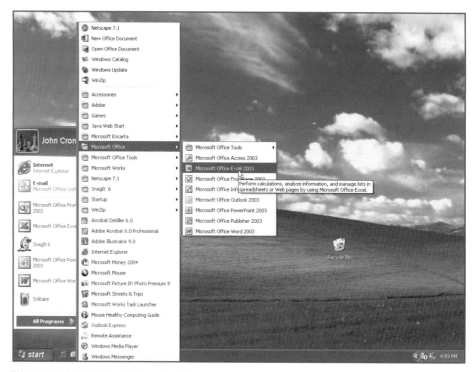

QUICKSTEPS

STARTING EXCEL

LOAD EXCEL FROM THE KEYBOARD

1. Press the Windows flag key, or press **CTRL+ESC**.

2. Press **P** to select the **All Programs** menu, and press **RIGHT-ARROW** to open it.

3. Press **DOWN-ARROW** until Microsoft Office is selected; press **RIGHT-ARROW** to open it.

4. Press **DOWN-ARROW** until **Microsoft Office Excel** is selected; press **ENTER** to load it.

CREATE A SHORTCUT TO START EXCEL

An alternative way to start Excel is to create a shortcut icon and to use it to start the program.

1. Open **Start**, select **All Programs**, choose **Microsoft Office**, and then press the right mouse button and drag **Microsoft Office Excel 2003** to one of the following:

- The upper-left "permanent" area of the Start menu

  —Or—

- The desktop

  —Or—

- The Quick Launch toolbar on the left end of the Taskbar next to Start (If you don't have a Quick Launch toolbar, right-click a blank area of the taskbar, click **Properties**, and place a check mark next to **Show Quick Launch**.)

2. Release the right mouse button, and click **Copy Here** if asked.

Figure 1-1: Starting Excel from desktop menus

1. Start your computer if it is not running, and log on to Windows if necessary.

2. Click **Start**. The Start menu opens.

3. Select **All Programs**, choose Microsoft Office, and click **Microsoft Office Excel 2003**, as shown in Figure 1-1.

Open a Workbook

The container for Excel *spreadsheets*—the grid where numbers, text, and formulas reside and calculations are performed—is a file called a *workbook* with a default filename of Book1.xls. When Excel is started, a new workbook is created and displays a blank worksheet, as shown in Figure 1-2. Within Excel, you can create a new workbook from scratch, use a template that defines a design for a workbook, or open an existing workbook and modify it.

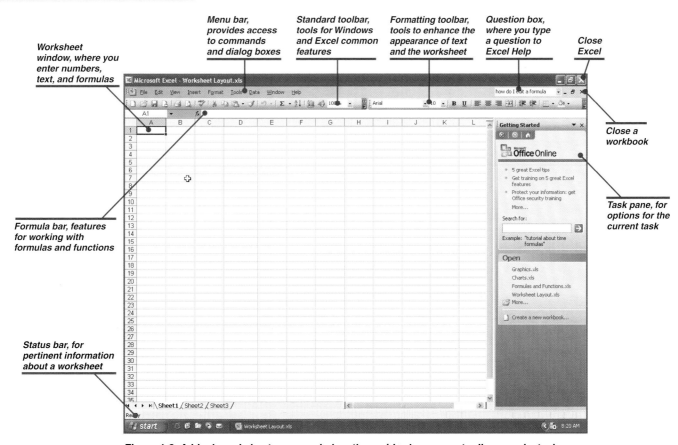

Menu bar, provides access to commands and dialog boxes

Standard toolbar, tools for Windows and Excel common features

Formatting toolbar, tools to enhance the appearance of text and the worksheet

Question box, where you type a question to Excel Help

Close Excel

Worksheet window, where you enter numbers, text, and formulas

Close a workbook

Task pane, for options for the current task

Formula bar, features for working with formulas and functions

Status bar, for pertinent information about a worksheet

Figure 1-2: A blank worksheet, surrounded on three sides by menus, toolbars, and a task pane, is the main focus of a new Excel workbook

CREATE A NEW WORKBOOK

When Excel is started, you can just start typing in the spreadsheet and workbook that is displayed, you can create another workbook, or you can choose from other options.

Figure 1-3: The New Workbook task pane provides several ways to create a new workbook

1. Open **File** and select **New**. The New Workbook task pane, shown in Figure 1-3, is displayed.

2. Select from the following:

   - **Blank Workbook** allows you to create one or more worksheets from scratch.

   - **Existing Workbook** brings up the New From Existing Workbook dialog box, where you can browse for an existing workbook. Then you can modify it to suit your current purposes.

   - **Templates** provides several ways to locate a prebuilt workbook, which you can open, save as a new workbook, and use as is or modify according to your needs.

OPEN AN EXISTING WORKBOOK

When you know the location of the workbook, to open it:

1. Open **File** and select **Open**.

2. In the Open dialog box, you can open the **Look In** drop-down list or click **My Recent Documents**, **Desktop**, **My Documents**, **My Computer**, or **My Network Places**, and then you can browse until you find the workbook you want.

3. When you have located it, double-click the workbook to open it.

Figure 1-4: The Open dialog box allows you to browse to find a workbook

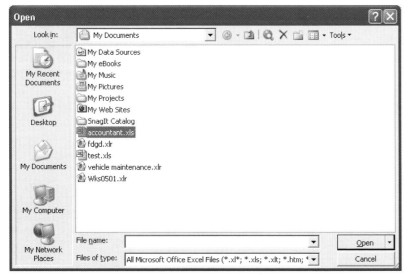

UICKSTEPS

OPENING A WORKBOOK

OPEN THE NEW WORKBOOK TASK PANE FROM THE KEYBOARD

In Excel, press **CTRL+N**.

OPEN A WORKBOOK WHEN OUTSIDE EXCEL

From the desktop, My Computer, or Windows Explorer:

- Drag the workbook file onto the Excel screen.

  –Or–

- Double-click the workbook file name or icon.

OPEN THE OPEN DIALOG BOX FROM THE KEYBOARD

In Excel, press **CTRL+O**.

TIP

To return to your previous workbook after either creating a new workbook or opening an existing one, click the minimized workbook shown as a task on the Windows taskbar, or select the **Excel Window** menu and click the workbook name.

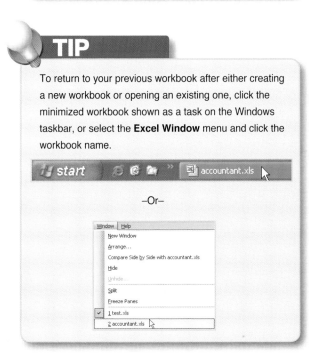

Add Identifying Information

You can add identifying information to a workbook to make it easier to find.

1. Open **File** and select **Properties**.

2. Type identifying information, such as Title, Subject, and Keywords (words or phrases that are associated with the workbook).

Figure 1-5:
You can more easily locate a workbook using search tools if you add identifying data

2004 Taxes.xls Properties

General | Summary | Statistics | Contents | Custom

Title:	2004 Federal Tax Data
Subject:	2004 Taxes
Author:	John Cronan
Manager:	Martin Matthews
Company:	Acme
Category:	
Keywords:	federal 2004 taxes income expenses deductions
Comments:	
Hyperlink base:	
Template:	

☐ Save preview picture

OK | Cancel

Find a Workbook

To find a workbook whose name and location you have forgotten, although you remember other information about it:

1. Open **File** and select **File Search**. The Basic File Search task pane opens, as shown in Figure 1-6.

2. In Search Text, type words you know the workbook contains or keywords (words or phrases associated with the workbook).

3. Open **Search In**, and select a location to narrow the scope of your search.

4. Open **Results Should Be**, and *deselect*, or clear, all check boxes except Excel Files.

5. Click **Go**.

Figure 1-6: The Basic File Search task pane provides options for common search techniques and a link to more advanced search features

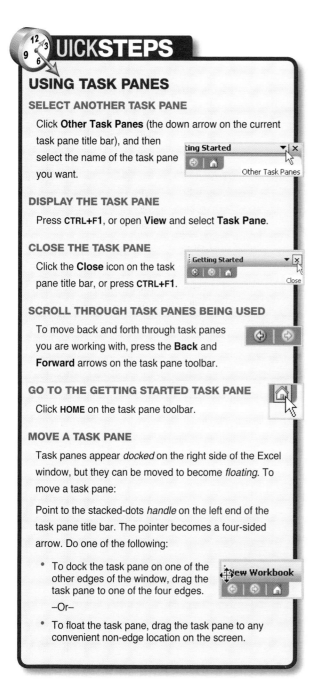

QUICKSTEPS

USING TASK PANES

SELECT ANOTHER TASK PANE

Click **Other Task Panes** (the down arrow on the current task pane title bar), and then select the name of the task pane you want.

DISPLAY THE TASK PANE

Press **CTRL+F1**, or open **View** and select **Task Pane**.

CLOSE THE TASK PANE

Click the **Close** icon on the task pane title bar, or press **CTRL+F1**.

SCROLL THROUGH TASK PANES BEING USED

To move back and forth through task panes you are working with, press the **Back** and **Forward** arrows on the task pane toolbar.

GO TO THE GETTING STARTED TASK PANE

Click **HOME** on the task pane toolbar.

MOVE A TASK PANE

Task panes appear *docked* on the right side of the Excel window, but they can be moved to become *floating*. To move a task pane:

Point to the stacked-dots *handle* on the left end of the task pane title bar. The pointer becomes a four-sided arrow. Do one of the following:

* To dock the task pane on one of the other edges of the window, drag the task pane to one of the four edges.

  –Or–

* To float the task pane, drag the task pane to any convenient non-edge location on the screen.

Personalize Excel

You can personalize Excel by changing the display of task panes, toolbars, and menus.

Remove the Getting Started Task Pane

When you start Excel, the Getting Started task pane automatically appears. To hide it:

1. Open **Tools** and select **Options**.

2. Open the **View** tab.

3. Remove the checkmark next to **Startup Task Pane**.

Select a Toolbar to Display

To display a toolbar:

1. Open **View** and select **Toolbars**. The Toolbars menu will be displayed, as shown in Figure 1-7.

2. Click the toolbar you want to display. A check mark is placed next to it, and the toolbar displays on the screen.

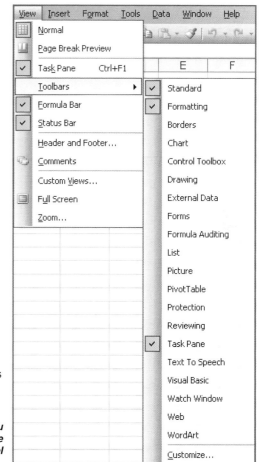

Figure 1-7: The Toolbars menu displays the toolbars available to be displayed in Excel

Show Toolbars on Two Rows

By default, the Standard and Formatting toolbars appear on one row with several of each toolbar's buttons typically hidden from view. To place the toolbars on two rows:

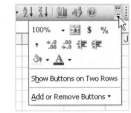

- Click **Toolbar Options** (the down arrow at the right end of a toolbar), and select **Show Buttons On Two Rows**.

  –Or–

- Open Tools and select **Customize**. Open the **Options** tab, and click **Show Standard And Formatting Toolbars On Two Rows**.

  –Or–

Drag the toolbar to the second row. (See the "Using Toolbars" QuickSteps for more information on moving toolbars.)

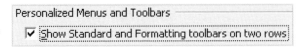

Customize a Toolbar

You can customize a toolbar or menu by adding commands or menus to it or by creating a new toolbar and adding commands to that.

ADD COMMANDS TO THE TOOLBAR

If you find the buttons on the toolbars are not as convenient as you would like or you frequently use a feature that is not on one of the toolbars, you can rearrange the buttons or add commands to a toolbar.

1. Open **Tools**, select **Customize**, and click the **Commands** tab.
2. Under Categories, select the category where the command will be found.

3. Under Commands, find the command, and drag it from the dialog box to the location on the toolbar where you want it.

4. Click **Close** when you are finished.

CREATE A CUSTOM TOOLBAR

You can create a custom toolbar with the commands on it that you most frequently use, avoid displaying several toolbars, and make more open space for the presentation. Here's how:

1. Open **Tools**, select **Customize**, and click the **Toolbars** tab.

2. Click **New**. The New Toolbar dialog box will be displayed.

3. Enter the name of the new toolbar, and click **OK**. A small toolbar will appear on the screen with the first few letters of its name in the title bar.

4. Use the steps in "Add Commands to the Toolbar" to build the toolbar with the commands you want.

DRAG A MENU TO A TOOLBAR

Excel provides several menus you can add to a custom or existing toolbar.

1. Open **Tools** and select **Customize**.

2. Open the **Commands** tab, and select **Built-in Menus** from the Categories list.

3. Drag the menu you want to the destination toolbar. See "Add Commands to the Tool-bar," earlier in this chapter, for steps on how to move commands.

QUICKSTEPS

USING TOOLBARS

DISPLAY A TOOLBAR

Right-click a toolbar or the menu bar, and click the toolbar you want to be displayed.

MOVE A TOOLBAR

- When the toolbar is docked (attached to the edge of a window), place your pointer on the handle on the left of the toolbar, and drag it to the new location.

- When the toolbar is floating, place your pointer on the title bar of the toolbar, and drag it to the new location.

HIDE A TOOLBAR

1. Right-click the toolbar.
2. Click the toolbar to remove the checkmark.

DELETE A TOOLBAR

You can delete only custom toolbars that you created.

1. Open **Tools**, select **Customize**, and click the **Toolbars** tab.
2. Click the check box next to the toolbar you want to delete.
3. Click **Delete**. You will be asked if you really want to delete the toolbar.
4. Click **OK** and click **Close**.

TIP

When you drag a toolbar next to the edge of the window, it will automatically attach itself to the window and become docked.

Get Help

Microsoft provides a vast amount of assistance to Excel users. Automatically sensing whether there is an Internet connection, Excel tailors much of the assistance offered to whether you are working online or offline.

Open Help

You are never far from help on Excel. Access it using one of these techniques:

DISPLAY THE EXCEL HELP TASK PANE

The Excel task pane, shown in Figure 1-8, provides links to several assistance tools and forums, including a table of contents, access to downloads, contact information, and late-breaking news on Excel. To display the Excel Help task pane:

- Open **Help**, and select **Microsoft Office Excel Help**.

  –Or–

- Click the **Microsoft Office Excel Help** icon on the Standard toolbar.

  –Or–

- Press **F1**.

Figure 1-8: The Excel Help task pane provides links to several avenues of online and offline assistance

QUICKSTEPS

USING HELP

PRINT A HELP TOPIC

Click the **Print** icon in the Help topic dialog box toolbar.

HIDE/SHOW THE OFFICE ASSISTANT

Open **Help**, and select **Hide The Office Assistant** or **Show The Office Assistant**, depending on whether you want to hide or show it.

NOTE

When you remove the display of the Office Assistant or the Type A Question For Help box, you are not deleting it, you are just hiding it.

NOTE

When you are working offline, only the reference tools provided with Excel, such as a thesaurus, are available.

TIP

The Research task pane is available from many context menus. Right-click the object of interest, and select **Look Up** from the menu.

ASK A QUESTION

You can quickly ask questions about Excel directly from the menu bar without use of the Excel Help task pane.

1. Type the question you want answered in the **Type A Question For Help** text box.

> Type a question for help ▾

2. Press **ENTER**.

HIDE THE TYPE A QUESTION FOR HELP BOX

To remove the display of the Type a Question For Help box:

1. Open **Tools** and select **Customize**. The Customize dialog box will open.
2. With the dialog box open, right-click the **Type A Question For Help** box on the menu bar.
3. Click the check mark beside the **Show Ask A Question** box, removing the checkmark.
4. Click **Close** on the dialog box. When the dialog box is closed, the text box will have been removed from the menu bar.

Do Research

Doing research on the Internet using Excel's Research command, which displays the Research task pane, allows you to enter your search criteria and specify references.

1. Open **Tools** and select **Research**.
2. Enter your search criteria in the **Search For** text box.
3. Beneath the text box, a reference source is selected. To change the reference source, open the list box and click a reference to be searched.
4. Click the **Go** arrow.

End Your Excel Workbook

When you are finished with your work, you need to save the workbook and close Excel. One way to make this more efficient is to get Excel to do it automatically while you work.

Save a Workbook Automatically

As you work with a workbook, it is important to periodically save it. Having Excel do it automatically will reduce the chance of losing data in case of a power failure or other interruption. To save your file automatically:

1. Open **Tools** and select **Options**.
2. Click the **Save** tab.
3. Click **Save AutoRecover Info Every** to place a check mark next to it.
4. In the Minutes box, enter a time specifying how often Excel is to save your workbook.

Save A Workbook Manually

Even if you use automatic saving, it's a good practice to manually save your workbook after you have done any significant work. To save a workbook file:

- Open **File** and click **Save**.

  –Or–

- Click the **Save** button on the Standard toolbar.

  –Or–

- Press **CTRL+S**.

TIP

Click to remove the **checkmark** next to **Save AutoRecover Info Every** if you want to stop the automatic saving of your workbooks.

NOTE

When you first open Excel, a default save interval of 10 minutes is set. Use the steps in "Save a Workbook Automatically" to change the default save interval to another time internval.

TIP

If this is your first time saving the file, the Save As dialog box will open. Type the name of the workbook in the **File Name** box, open the **Save In** box (or use the icons along the left side of the dialog box), and browse until you find the location where you want the file saved.

COPYING AND MOVING FILES AND FOLDERS

Copying and moving files and folders can be done to some degree within Excel, but it is often more efficient to do file and folder management in the Windows Explorer. To open the Explorer, open the **Start** menu, select **All Programs**, choose **Accessories**, and click **Windows Explorer**.

COPY WITH THE MOUSE

To copy with the mouse, press and hold **CTRL** while dragging a file or folder from one folder to another on the same disk drive or while dragging a file or folder from one disk drive to another.

MOVE NON-PROGRAM FILES ON THE SAME DISK WITH THE MOUSE

Move non-program files from one folder to another on the same disk with the mouse by dragging the file or folder.

MOVE NON-PROGRAM FILES TO ANOTHER DISK WITH THE MOUSE

Move non-program files to another disk by pressing and holding **SHIFT** while dragging them.

MOVE PROGRAM FILES WITH THE MOUSE

Move program files to another folder or disk by pressing and holding **SHIFT** while dragging them.

COPY AND MOVE WITH THE MOUSE AND A MENU

To copy and move with a mouse and a menu, press and hold the right-mouse button while dragging the file or folder. When you release the right-mouse button, a context menu opens that allows you to choose whether to copy, move, or create a shortcut.

Continued...

Save a Copy of Your Workbook

When you save a workbook under a different name, you create a copy of it. Both the original workbook and the newly named one will remain. To create a copy with a new name:

1. Open **File** and choose **Save As**.

2. In the Save As dialog box, as shown in Figure 1-9, type a **File Name**, and then open the **Save In** box (or use the icons along the left side of the dialog box), and browse until you find the location where you want the file saved.

3. Click **Save**.

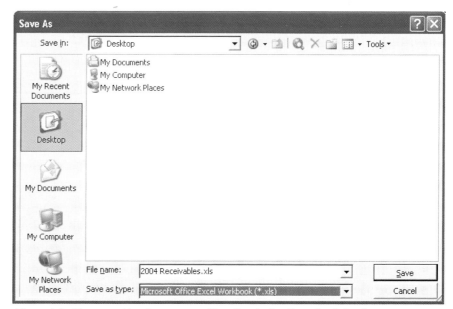

Figure 1-9: Give a workbook a name and location in the Save As dialog box

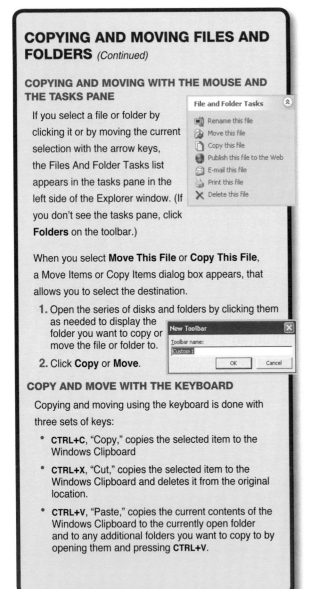

COPYING AND MOVING FILES AND FOLDERS *(Continued)*

COPYING AND MOVING WITH THE MOUSE AND THE TASKS PANE

If you select a file or folder by clicking it or by moving the current selection with the arrow keys, the Files And Folder Tasks list appears in the tasks pane in the left side of the Explorer window. (If you don't see the tasks pane, click **Folders** on the toolbar.)

File and Folder Tasks
- Rename this file
- Move this file
- Copy this file
- Publish this file to the Web
- E-mail this file
- Print this file
- Delete this file

When you select **Move This File** or **Copy This File**, a Move Items or Copy Items dialog box appears, that allows you to select the destination.

1. Open the series of disks and folders by clicking them as needed to display the folder you want to copy or move the file or folder to.

2. Click **Copy** or **Move**.

COPY AND MOVE WITH THE KEYBOARD

Copying and moving using the keyboard is done with three sets of keys:

- **CTRL+C**, "Copy," copies the selected item to the Windows Clipboard
- **CTRL+X**, "Cut," copies the selected item to the Windows Clipboard and deletes it from the original location.
- **CTRL+V**, "Paste," copies the current contents of the Windows Clipboard to the currently open folder and to any additional folders you want to copy to by opening them and pressing **CTRL+V**.

Save a Workbook As a Template

To save a workbook as a template so that you can create new workbooks and worksheets from it:

1. Create a workbook. The remaining chapters in this book show you how to do this.
2. Open **File** and select **Save As**.
3. Enter a **File Name** for your template.
4. In the **Save As Type** box, select **Template**.
5. Browse to a location, or use the shortcuts on the left side of the dialog box.
6. Click **Save**.

Close an Excel Session

After you have saved the most recent changes to your workbook, you can close the workbook and then exit Excel.

CLOSE THE WORKBOOK

1. Open **File** and choose **Close**, or click the Close Window button on the workbook menu bar.
2. Click **Yes** to save the workbook when asked.

CLOSE EXCEL

- Open **File** and select **Exit**, or click **Close**.

How to...

- Enter Text
- *Completing an Entry*
- Enter Numeric Data
- *Formatting Numbers*
- Enter Dates
- Use Times
- *Adding Data Quickly*
- Edit Cell Data
- Remove Cell Contents
- *Selecting Cells and Ranges*
- Copy and Paste Data
- Use Paste Special
- Find and Replace Data
- Verify Spelling
- Modify Automatic Corrections

Chapter 2
Entering and Editing Data

Data is the heart and soul of Excel, yet before we can calculate data, chart it, analyze it, and otherwise *use* it, we have to place it on a worksheet. Data comes in several forms—such as numbers, text, dates, and times—and Excel handles the entry of each form uniquely. After you enter data into Excel's worksheets, you might want to make changes or verify accuracy, so Excel offers automatic tools to assist you along the way.

Enter Data

An Excel worksheet is a matrix, or grid, of lettered *column headers* across its top and numbered *row headers* down its side. The first row of a typical worksheet is used for column *headings*. The column headings represent categories of similar data. The rows beneath a column heading contain data further categorized by a row heading along the leftmost column, or listed below the column heading. Figure 2-1 shows examples of two common worksheet arrangements. Worksheets can also be used to set up databases, where columns are referred to as *fields* and each row represents a unique *record* of data. Databases are covered in Chapter 8.

NOTE

The terms "spreadsheet" and "worksheet" can be used interchangeably. They both refer to a grid of columns and rows that contain data upon which you can perform calculations.

Each intersection of a row and column is called a *cell* and is referenced first by its column location and then by its row location. The combination of a column letter and row number assigns each cell an *address*. For example, the cell at the intersection of column D and row 8 is called D8. A cell is considered to be *active* when it is clicked or otherwise selected as the place in which to place new data.

Columns are identified by lettered headers across the top of the worksheet

Data organized by column and row headings

Column headings categorize data vertically

Data organized by column headings (or fields) and records

Rows are identified by numbered headers along the left side of the worksheet

Row headings categorize data horizontally

Active cell is ready to accept data

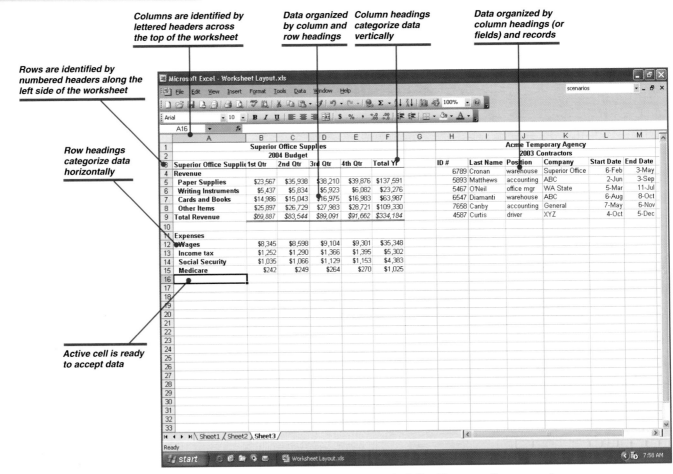

Figure 2-1: The grid layout of Excel worksheets is defined by several components

1 3 4 5 6 7 8 9 10

Enter Text

In an Excel worksheet, text is used to identify, explain, and emphasize numeric data. It comprises characters that cannot be used in calculations. You enter text by typing just as you would in a word processing program.

ENTER TEXT CONTINUOUSLY

Text (and numbers) longer than one cell width will appear to cover the adjoining cells to the right of the active cell. The covered cells have not been "used"; their contents have just been hidden, as shown in Figure 2-2. To enter text on one line:

1. Click the cell where you want the text to start.

2. Type the text. The text displays in one or more cells. (See Chapter 3, "Formatting a Worksheet," for information on changing cell width.)

3. Complete the entry. (See the QuickSteps, "Completing an Entry," for several ways to do that.)

Row and column headers are highlighted for active cell

Name box shows address of active cell

Active cell

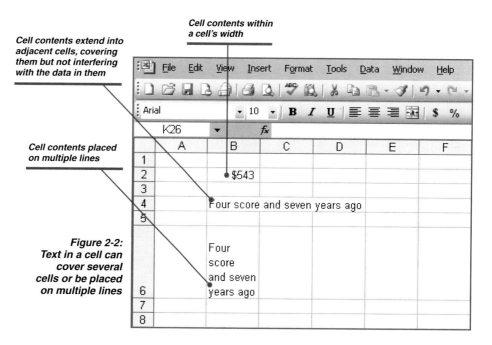

Cell contents within a cell's width

Cell contents extend into adjacent cells, covering them but not interfering with the data in them

Cell contents placed on multiple lines

Figure 2-2: Text in a cell can cover several cells or be placed on multiple lines

QUICKSTEPS

COMPLETING AN ENTRY

You can complete an entry, using the mouse or the keyboard, and control where the active cell goes next.

STAY IN THE ACTIVE CELL

To complete an entry and keep the current cell active, click **Enter** on the Formula bar. ✓

MOVE THE ACTIVE CELL TO THE RIGHT

To complete the entry and move to the next cell in the same row, press **TAB** or **RIGHT ARROW**.

$4,383
$1,025

MOVE THE ACTIVE CELL TO THE NEXT ROW

To complete the entry and move the active cell to the next row, press **ENTER**. The active cell moves to the beginning cell of the next row.

CHANGE THE DIRECTION OF THE ACTIVE CELL

1. Open **Tools**, select **Options**, and click the **Edit** tab. Under Settings, verify Move Selection After Enter is checked.

2. Open the **Direction** drop-down list box and click a direction. Down is the default.

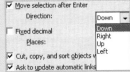

3. Close the Options dialog box.

MOVE THE ACTIVE CELL TO ANY CELL

To complete the entry and move the active cell to any cell in the worksheet:

- Click the cell you want to become active.

  –Or–

- Press one of the four arrow keys one or more times in the direction of the cell you want to activate until you have reached that cell.

ENTER TEXT ON MULTIPLE LINES

When you want to constrain the length of text in a cell or otherwise display text on more than one line in a cell:

1. Click the cell where you want the text.
2. Type the text you want to appear on the first line.
3. Press **ALT+ENTER**. The insertion point moves to the beginning of a new line.
4. Repeat Steps 2 and 3 for any additional lines of text. (See Figure 2-2)
5. Complete the entry. (See the QuickSteps, "Completing an Entry.")

Enter Numeric Data

Numbers are numerical data, from the simplest to the most complex. Excel provides several features to help you more easily work with numbers used to represent values in various categories, such as currency, accounting, and mathematics.

ENTER NUMBERS

Enter numbers by simply selecting a cell and typing the numbers.

1. Click the cell where you want the numbers entered.
2. Type the numbers. Use decimal places, thousands separators, and other formatting as you type, or have Excel format for you. (See the QuickSteps, "Formatting Numbers.")
3. Complete the entry. (See the QuickSteps, "Completing an Entry.")

ENTER NUMBERS USING SCIENTIFIC NOTATION

Exponents are used in scientific notation to shorten (or round off) very large or small numbers. The shorthand scientific notation display does not affect how the number is used in calculations.

1. Click the cell where you want the data entered.

NOTE

The *beginning cell* is in the same column where you first started entering data. For example, if you started entering data in cell A5 and continued through E5, pressing **TAB** between entries A5 through D5 and **ENTER** in E5, the active cell would move to A6 (the first cell in the next row). If you had started entering data in cell C5, after pressing **ENTER** at the end of that row of entries the active cell would move to C6, the cell below it.

TIP

You can cause a number to be interpreted by Excel as text by typing an apostrophe (') in front of the number and completing the entry. The "number" is left aligned as text and a green triangle is displayed in the upper-left corner of the cell. When selected, an error icon displays next to the cell indicating a number is stored as text.

TIP

You can convert a number to scientific notation by selecting the cell and opening **Format**, selecting **Cells** and choosing the **Number** tab. Click the **Scientific** category and use the *spinner* (the increase and decrease arrows to the right of the text box) to set the number of Decimal Places.

2. Type the number using three components:

- **Base**. For example: 4, 7.56, -2.5

- **Scientific notation identifier**. Type the letter "e."

- **Exponent**. The number of 10s places the entry represents positive numbers to the left of the decimal point, negative numbers to the right.

   For example, scientific notation for the number 123,456,789.0 is written to two decimal places as 1.23×10^8. In Excel you would type 1.23e8, and it would display as: 1.23E+08

3. Complete the entry. (See the QuickSteps, "Completing an Entry.")

Enter Dates

If you can think of a way to enter a date, Excel can probably recognize it as such. For example, to use the date of March 1st 2004 (assuming it is sometime in 2004) in a worksheet, Table 2-1 shows how Excel handles different ways to make the date entry.

In cases when a year is omitted Excel assumes the current year.

TABLE 2-1: *Example Excel Date Formats*

TYPING THIS...	DISPLAYS THIS AFTER COMPLETING THE ENTRY...
3/1, 3-1, 1-mar, or 1-Mar	1-Mar
3/1/04, 3-1-04, 3/1/2004, 3-1-2004 3-1/04, or 3-1/2004	3/1/2004
Mar 1, 04, March 1, 2004, 1-mar-04, or 1-Mar-2004	1-Mar-04

UICKSTEPS

FORMATTING NUMBERS

Numbers in a cell can be formatted for any one of several numeric categories by first selecting the cell containing the number, then opening **Format**, selecting **Cells,** and choosing the **Number** tab, shown in Figure 2-3.

ADD DECIMAL PLACES

1. On the Format Cells dialog box Number tab, choose the appropriate numeric category (Number, Currency, Accounting, Percentage, or Scientific) from the Category list box.

2. In the Decimal Places text box, enter a number or use the spinner to set the number of decimal places you want. Click **OK**.

ADD A THOUSANDS SEPARATOR

On the Format Cells dialog box Number tab, click **Use 1000 Separator (,)**. Click **OK**.

ADD A CURRENCY SYMBOL

1. On the Format Cells dialog box Number tab, choose the appropriate numeric category (Currency or Accounting) from the Category list box.

2. Click **OK** to accept the default dollar sign ($) or choose another currency symbol from the Symbol drop-down list and click **OK**.

LINE UP CURRENCY SYMBOLS AND DECIMALS IN A COLUMN

1. On the Format Cells dialog box Number tab, click the **Accounting** category.

2. Select the number of decimal places and the currency symbol you want. Click **OK**.

CONVERT DECIMAL TO FRACTIONS

1. On the Format Cells dialog box Number tab, click the **Fraction** category.

Continued...

CHANGE THE DEFAULT DISPLAY OF DATES

Dates are displayed by default in Excel from settings in the Regional And Language Options control panel, shown in Figure 2-4. In Excel, you can tell what short date setting is currently in use by clicking a cell with a date in it and seeing what appears in the Formula bar.

fx 3/5/2004

You can change the default settings by:

1. Opening **Start** and clicking **Control Panel**.

2. Depending on which view of the Control Panel you are using:

   - In Category View, click the **Date, Time, Language, And Regional Options** category, and then click **Regional And Language Options**.

   –Or–

   - In Classic View, double-click **Regional And Language Options**.

3. On the Regional Options tab, click **Customize**.

4. Click the **Date** tab, open the **Short Date Format** drop-down list box, and select a format.

5. Similarly select a date separator and a long date format.

6. Click **OK** twice and close the **Control Panel**.

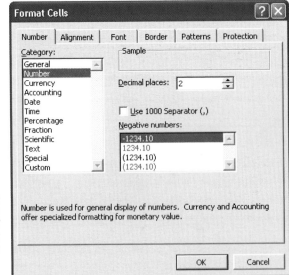

Figure 2-3: The Format Cells Number tab provides several numeric formatting categories

FORMATTING NUMBERS *(Continued)*

2. Click the type of fraction you want. View it in the Sample area and change the type if needed. Click **OK**.

CONVERT NUMBERS TO SCIENTIFIC NOTATION

1. On the Format Cells dialog box Number tab, click the **Scientific** category.

2. In the Decimal Places text box, enter a number or use the spinner to set the number of decimal places you want. Click **OK**.

   (For more information on scientific notation, see "Enter Numbers Using Scientific Notation" earlier in this chapter.)

CONVERT A NUMBER TO A PERCENTAGE

1. On the Format Cells dialog box Number tab, click the **Percentage** category.

2. In the Decimal Places text box, enter a number or use the spinner to set the number of decimal places you want. Click **OK**.

FORMAT ZIP CODES, PHONE NUMBERS, AND SSNS

1. On the Format Cells dialog box Number tab, click the **Special** category.

2. Select the **Type** of formatting you want. Click **OK**.

NOTE

Formatting also can be applied to cells in advance of entering numbers (or text) so the attributes are displayed as you complete the entry. Simply select the cells and apply the formatting. See the QuickSteps "Selecting Cells and Ranges" for ways to select cells.

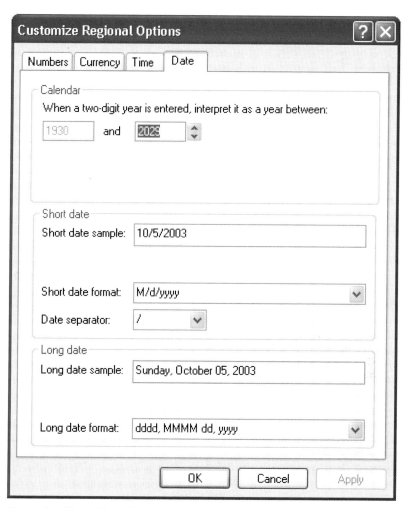

Figure 2-4: Change how Excel and other Windows applications display dates

FORMAT DATES

You can change how a date is displayed in Excel by choosing a new format.

1. Select the cell that contains the date you want to change. (See the QuickSteps "Selecting Cells and Ranges" to see how to apply formats to more than one cell at a time.)

2. Open **Format**, select **Cells**, and click the **Number** tab. The Format Cells dialog box Number tab opens, as shown in Figure 2-3.

3. Click the **Date** category and select a format. You can see how the new date format affects your date in the Sample area. Click **OK** when finished.

To enter the current date in a cell, click the cell and type **CTRL+;** (press and hold **CTRL** and press **;**). The current date in the form mm/ddd/yyyy is displayed.

Use Times

Excel's conventions for time:

● Colons (:) are used as separators between hours, minutes, and seconds.

● AM is assumed unless you specify PM or when you enter a time from 12:00 to 12:59.

● AM and PM do not display in the cell if they are not entered.

● You specify PM by entering a space followed by "p," "P," "pm," or "PM."

● Seconds are not displayed in the cell if not entered.

● AM, PM, and seconds are displayed in the Formula bar of a cell that contains a time.

ENTER TIMES

1. Select the cell in which you want to enter a time.

2. Type the hour followed by a colon.

3. Type the minutes followed by a colon.

4. Type the seconds, if needed.

5. Type a space and **PM**, if needed.

6. Complete the entry.

CHANGE THE DEFAULT DISPLAY OF TIMES

Times are displayed by default in Excel from settings in the Regional And Language Options control panel. To change the default settings:

1. Open **Start** and click **Control Panel**.

2. Depending on the view you have:

   • In Category View, click the **Date**, **Time**, **Language**, **And Regional Options** category, and then click **Regional And Language Options**.

   –Or–

   • In Classic View, double-click **Regional And Language Options**.

3. On the Regional Options tab, click **Customize**.

4. Click the **Time** tab, open the **Time Format** drop-down list box, and select a format. The choices are whether to include seconds or use a 24-hour clock (capital H).

5. Click **OK** twice and close the **Control Panel**.

To enter the current time in a cell, click the cell and type **CTRL+SHIFT+:**. The current time in the form h:mm AM/PM is displayed.

CAUTION

Changing the *system* date/time formats in **Regional And Language Options** changes date and time formats used by all Windows programs. Dates and times previously entered in Excel may change to the new setting unless they were formatted using the features in Excel's Format Cells dialog box.

ADDING DATA QUICKLY

Excel provides several features that help you quickly add more data to existing data with a minimum of keystrokes.

USE AUTOCOMPLETE

Excel will complete an entry for you after you type the first few characters of data that appears in a previous entry in the same column. Simply press **ENTER** to accept the completed entry. To turn off this feature if you find it bothersome:

Position	Company
warehouse	Superior Office
accounting	ABC
office mgr	WA State
warehouse	ABC
accounting	General
driver	XYZ
office mgr	

1. Open **Tools**, select **Options**, and click the **Edit** tab.
2. Click **Enable AutoComplete For Cell Values** to remove the checkmark.

☑ Enable AutoComplete for cell values

FILL DATA INTO ADJOINING CELLS

1. Select the cell that contains the data you want to copy into adjoining cells.
2. Point to the fill handle in the lower-right corner of the cell. The pointer becomes a single line cross.
3. Drag the handle in the direction you want to extend the data until you've reached the last cell in the range you want to fill.
4. Open the Smart tag and select fill options.

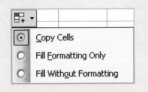

○ Copy Cells
○ Fill Formatting Only
○ Fill Without Formatting

Continued...

FORMAT TIMES

You can change how a time is displayed in Excel by choosing a new format.

1. Select the cell that contains the time you want to change. (See the QuickSteps "Selecting Cells and Ranges" for how to apply formats to more than one cell at a time.)
2. Open **Format**, select **Cells**, and click the **Number** tab. The Format Cells dialog box Number tab opens, as shown in Figure 2-3.
3. Click the **Time** category and select a format. You can see how the new time format will affect your time in the Sample area. Click **OK** when finished.

Edit Data

The data intensive manner of Excel necessitates easy ways to change, copy, or remove data already entered on a worksheet. Additionally, Excel has facilities to help you find and replace data and check its spelling.

Edit Cell Data

You have several choices on how to edit data, depending on whether you want to replace all the contents of a cell or just part of the contents, and whether you want to do it in the cell or in the Formula bar.

EDIT CELL CONTENTS

To edit data entered in a cell:

- Double-click the text in the cell where you want to begin editing. An insertion point is placed in the cell. Type the new data or use the mouse to select characters to be overwritten or deleted, or use keyboard shortcuts. Complete the entry when finished editing. (See the QuickSteps, "Completing an Entry.")

–Or–

ADDING DATA QUICKLY *(Continued)*

CONTINUE A SERIES OF DATA

Data can be *logically* extended into one or more adjoining cells. For example, 1 and 2 extend to 3, 4...; Tuesday extends to Wednesday, Thursday...; January extends to February, March...; and 2004 and 2005 extend to 2006, 2007....

1. Select the cell or cells that contain a partial series. (See the QuickSteps "Selecting Cells and Ranges" for more information on selecting more than one cell.)

2. Point to the fill handle in the lower-right corner of the last cell. The pointer becomes a single line cross.

3. Drag the handle in the direction you want until you've reached the last cell in the range to complete the series.

| january |
| february |
| march |
| april |
| may |
| june |
| july |

REMOVE THE FILL HANDLE

To hide the fill handle and disable AutoFill:

1. Open **Tools**, select **Options**, and click the **Edit** tab.

2. Click **Allow Cell Drag And Drop** to remove the check mark.

ENTER DATA FROM A LIST

Previously entered data in a column is available to be selected from a list and entered with a click.

1. Right-click the cell at the bottom of a column of data.

2. Select **Pick From Drop-Down List** from the context menu and then click the data you want to enter in the cell.

| Last Name |
| Cronan |
| Matthews |
| O'Neil |
| Diamanti |
| Canby |
| Curtis |

| Canby |
| Cronan |
| Curtis |
| Diamanti |
| Last Name |
| Matthews |
| O'Neil |

TIP

You can fill data into the active cell from the cell above or to its right by clicking **CTRL+D** or **CTRL+R,** respectively.

- Select the cell to edit and then click the cell's contents in the Formula bar where you want to make changes. Type the new data or use the mouse to select characters to overwrite or delete, or use keyboard shortcuts. Click **Enter** on the Formula bar or press **Enter** to complete the entry.

  X ✓ *fx* janﬞary

  –Or–

- Select the cell to edit and press **F2**. Edit in the cell or on the Formula bar using the mouse or keyboard shortcuts. Complete the entry.

REPLACE ALL CELL CONTENTS

Click the cell and type new data. The original data is deleted and replaced by your new characters.

CANCEL CELL EDITING

Before you complete a cell entry, you can revert back to your original data by pressing **ESC** or clicking **Cancel** on the Formula bar. ☒

Remove Cell Contents

You can easily delete cell contents, move them to other cells, or clear selective attributes of a cell.

DELETE DATA

Remove all contents (but not formatting) from a cell by selecting it and pressing **DELETE**. You can delete the contents of more than one cell by selecting the cells or range and pressing **DELETE**. (See the QuickSteps "Selecting Cells and Ranges" for more information on selecting various configurations.)

MOVE DATA

Cell contents can be removed from one location and placed in another location of equal size. Select the cell or range you want to move and then:

UICKSTEPS

SELECTING CELLS AND RANGES

Key to many actions in Excel is the ability to select cells in various configurations and use them to perform calculations. You can select a single cell, non-adjacent cells, and adjacent cells (or *ranges*).

SELECT A SINGLE CELL

Select a cell by clicking it, or move to a cell using the arrow keys or by completing an entry in an adjacent cell.

SELECT NON-ADJACENT CELLS

Select a cell and then press **CTRL** while clicking the other cells you want to select.

SELECT A RANGE OF ADJACENT CELLS

Select a cell and drag over the additional cells you want to include in the range.

SELECT ALL CELLS ON A WORKSHEET

Click the **Select All** "button" in the upper-left corner of the worksheet or press **CTRL+A**.

SELECT A ROW OR COLUMN

Click a row header or column header.

SELECT ADJACENT ROWS OR COLUMNS

Drag down the row headers or across the column headers.

Continued...

- Place the pointer on any edge of the selection, except the lower-right corner, until it turns into a cross with arrowhead tips. Drag the cell or range to the new location.

  –Or–

- Open **Edit** and select **Cut**, or click **Cut** on the Standard toolbar. Select the new location and open **Edit** and select **Paste**, or click **Paste** on the Standard toolbar. (See "Copy and Paste Data" later in this chapter for more information on using the Windows Clipboard.)

REMOVE CELL CONTENTS SELECTIVELY

A cell can contain several components, including:

- **Formats**, consisting of number formats, conditional formats (formats that display if certain conditions apply), and borders
- **Contents**, consisting of formulas and data
- **Comments**, consisting of notes you attach to a cell

Choose which cell components you want to clear by selecting the cell or cells, opening **Edit**, pointing to **Clear**, and clicking the applicable item from the subsidiary menu.

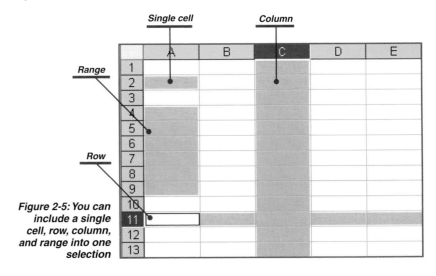

Figure 2-5: You can include a single cell, row, column, and range into one selection

Copy and Paste Data

Data you've already entered on a worksheet can be copied to the same or other worksheets, or even to other Windows applications (see Chapter 10 for information on using data with other programs). You first *copy* the data to the Windows Clipboard, where it is temporarily stored. After selecting a destination for the data, you *paste* it into the cell or cells. You can copy all the data in a cell or you can select only part of it.

1. Select the cells that contain the data you want to copy, or double-click a cell and select the characters you want to copy.

2. Open **Edit** and select **Copy**, or click **Copy** on the Standard toolbar, or press **CTRL+C**. The selected data is copied to the Clipboard and the border around the cells displays a flashing dotted line.

3. Select the new location for the data. Then either open **Edit** and select **Paste,** or click **Paste** on the Standard toolbar, or press **CTRL+V**. The selected data is entered into the new cells.

4. Open the Smart tag next to the pasted data and choose the formatting or other options you want.

5. Repeat steps 3 and 4 to copy and paste to other locations. Press **ESC** when finished to remove the flashing border around the source cells.

Keep Source Formatting
Match Destination Formatting
Values and Number Formatting
Keep Source Column Widths
Formatting Only
Link Cells

Use Paste Special

Paste Special allows you to selectively include or omit formulas, values, formatting, comments, arithmetic operations, and other cell properties *before* you copy or move data. (See Chapter 4 for information on formulas, values, and arithmetic operations.) This tool offers more options than the Paste Options Smart tag used *after* you paste.

1. Select and then copy or cut the data you want.

TIP

To select larger numbers of adjacent cells, rows, or columns click the first item in the group and then press **SHIFT** while clicking the last item in the group.

CAUTION

If you use the Delete option on the Edit menu, you delete the selected cells from the worksheet *and* their contents. See Chapter 3 for information on deleting cells.

2. Select the destination cell or cells to where you want the data copied or moved.

3. Open **Edit** and click **Paste Special**, or right-click the destination cells and click **Paste Special**. The Paste Special dialog box opens, as shown in Figure 2-6.

4. Select the paste options you want in the copied or moved cells and click **OK**.

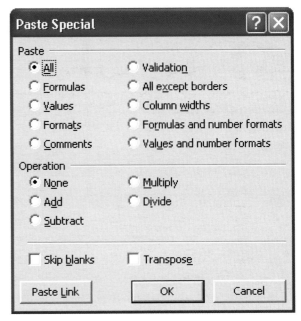

Figure 2-6: You can selectively add or omit many cell properties when you use the Paste Special dialog box to copy or move data

Find and Replace Data

In worksheets that might span thousands of rows and columns, you need the ability to locate data quickly as well as to find instances of the same data so consistent replacements can be made.

FIND DATA

1. Open **Edit** and select **Find**, or press **CTRL+F** to open the Find And Replace dialog box Find tab, shown in Figure 2-7.

2. Type the characters you want to find in the Find What text box.

3. Click **Options** to view the following options to refine the search:

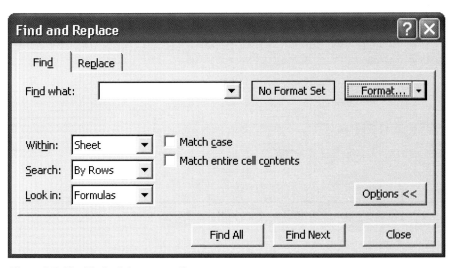

Figure 2-7: The Find tab lets you refine your search based on several criteria

- **Format**, opens the Find Format dialog box where you select from several categories of number, alignment, font, border, patterns, and protection formats.

- **Choose Format From Cell** (from the Format drop-down list), lets you click a cell that contains the format you want to find.

- **Within**, limits your search to the current worksheet or expands it all worksheets in the workbook.

- **Search**, lets you search to the right by rows or down by columns. You can reverse the direction of the search by pressing **SHIFT** and clicking **Find Next**.

- **Look In**, focuses the search to just formulas, values, or comments.

- **Match Case**, lets you choose between uppercase or lowercase text.

- **Match Entire Cell Contents**, searches for an exact match of the characters in Find What.

4. Click **Find All** to display a table of all occurrences or click **Find Next** to find the next singular occurrence.

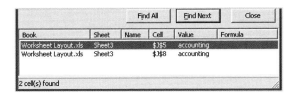

REPLACE DATA

The Replace tab of the Find And Replace dialog box looks and behaves similar to the Find tab covered earlier.

1. Open **Edit** and select **Replace,** or press **CTRL+H** to open the Find And Replace dialog box Replace tab.

2. Enter the characters to find in the Find What text box; enter the replacement characters in the Replace With text box. If formatting or search criteria are required, click **Options**. See "Find Data" for the options' descriptions.

3. Click **Replace All** to replace all occurrences in the worksheet or click **Replace** to replace occurrences one at a time.

Verify Spelling

You can check spelling of selected cells or the entire worksheet using Excel's main dictionary and a custom dictionary (both shared with other Office programs) you add words to.

1. Select the cells to check, or to check the entire worksheet select any cell.

2. Click **Spelling** on the Standard toolbar or open **Tools** and select **Spelling**. When the spell checker doesn't find anything to report, you are told the spelling check is complete. Otherwise, the Spelling dialog box opens as shown on Figure 2-8.

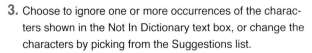

3. Choose to ignore one or more occurrences of the characters shown in the Not In Dictionary text box, or change the characters by picking from the Suggestions list.

4. Click **AutoCorrect** if you want to automatically replace words in the future. (See "Modify Automatic Corrections" later in this chapter for more information on using AutoCorrect.)

5. Click **Options** to change language or custom dictionaries and set other spelling criteria.

TIP

If the correct spelling of a misspelled word is not shown in the Suggestions list box, edit the word in the Not In Dictionary text box and click **Add To Dictionary** to include it in a custom dictionary that is checked in addition to the main dictionary.

Modify Automatic Corrections

Excel automatically corrects common data entry mistakes as you type, replacing characters and words you choose with other choices. You may control how this is done.

1. Open **Tools**, select **Options**, choose the **Spelling** tab, and click **AutoCorrect Options**. The AutoCorrect dialog box opens, as shown in Figure 2-9. As appropriate, do one or more of the following:

   • Choose the type of automatic corrections you do or do not want from the options at the top of the dialog box.

   • Click **Exceptions** to set capitalization exceptions.

   • Click **Replace Text As You Type** to turn off automatic text replacement (turned on by default).

   • Add new words or characters to the Replace and With lists and click **Add**, or select a current item in the list, edit it, and click **Replace**.

   • Delete replacement text by selecting the item in the Replace/With list and clicking **Delete**.

2. Click **OK** when you are done.

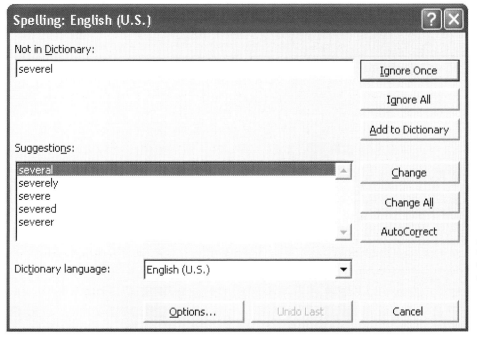

Figure 2-8: The Spelling dialog box provides several options to handle misspelled or uncommon words

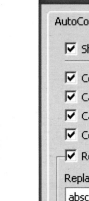

TIP

AutoCorrect lists (and other proofing tools, such as thesauri) are available on a single CD for more than 50 languages. Go to shop.microsoft.com and search for Office 2003 Proofing Tools.

Figure 2-9: AutoCorrect provides several automatic correction settings and lets you add words and characters that are replaced with alternates

How to...

Chapter 3
Formatting a Worksheet

In this chapter you will learn how to add and delete cells, rows, and columns, and how to change their appearance, both manually and by having Excel do it for you. You will see how to change the appearance of text, how to use styles for a more consistent look, and how to add comments to a cell to better explain important points. Techniques to better display worksheets are also covered.

Work with Cells, Rows, and Columns

Getting a worksheet to look the way you want will probably involve adding and removing cells, rows, or columns to appropriately separate your data and remove unwanted space. You will also want to adjust the size, type of border, and background of the cells from their default settings. This section covers these features and more.

QUICKSTEPS

ADDING AND REMOVING ROWS, COLUMNS, AND CELLS

You can insert or delete rows one at a time or select adjacent and non-adjacent rows to perform these actions on them together. (See the QuickSteps, "Selecting Ranges and Cells" in Chapter 2 for information on selecting rows, columns, and cells.)

ADD A SINGLE ROW

1. Click a cell in the row below where you want the new row.
2. Open **Insert** and click **Rows**.

ADD MULTIPLE ADJACENT ROWS

1. Select the number of rows you want immediately below the row where you want the new rows.
2. Open **Insert** and click **Rows**, or right-click the selection and click **Insert**.

ADD ROWS TO MULTIPLE NON-ADJACENT ROWS

1. Select the number of rows you want immediately below the first row where you want the new rows.
2. Press and hold **CTRL** while selecting the number of rows you want immediately below any other rows.
3. Open **Insert** and click **Rows**, or right-click any selection and click **Insert**.

ADD A SINGLE COLUMN

1. Click a cell in the column to the right of where you want the new column.
2. Open **Insert** and click **Columns**.

ADD MULTIPLE ADJACENT COLUMNS

1. Select the number of columns you want immediately to the right of column where you want the new columns.
2. Open **Insert** and click **Columns**, or right-click the selection and click **Insert**.

Continued...

Adjust Row Height

You can change the height of a row manually or by changing cell contents.

CHANGE THE HEIGHT FOR A SINGLE ROW

1. Point at the bottom border of the row header until the pointer changes to a cross with up and down arrowheads.

8	Other Items
9	Total Revenue
10	

2. Drag the border up or down to the row height you want.

CHANGE THE HEIGHT FOR MULTIPLE ROWS

1. Select the rows you want to adjust.
2. Open **Format**, point at **Row**, and click **Height**. The Row Height dialog box opens.

3. Type a new height in *points* (there are 72 points to an inch) and click **OK**. The cell height changes, but the size of the cell contents stays the same.

CHANGE ROW HEIGHT BY CHANGING CELL CONTENTS

1. Select one or more cells, rows, or characters that you want to change in height.
2. Change the cell contents. Some examples of the various ways to do this include:
   - To change font size, click the **Font Size** down arrow on the Formatting toolbar, and click a size from the drop-down list.
   - To place characters on two or more lines within a cell, place the insertion point at the end of a line and press **ALT+ENTER**.

ADDING AND REMOVING ROWS, COLUMNS, AND CELLS (Continued)

ADD COLUMNS TO MULTIPLE NON-ADJACENT COLUMNS

1. Select the number of columns you want immediately to the right of the first column where you want the new columns.

2. Press and hold **CTRL** while selecting the number of columns you want immediately to the right of any other columns.

3. Open **Insert** and click **Columns**, or right-click any selection and click **Insert**.

ADD CELLS

1. Select the cells near where you want to insert the new cells.

2. Open **Insert** and click **Cells**, or right-click the selection and click **Insert**.

3. In the Insert dialog box, choose the direction to shift the existing cells. Click **OK**.

ATTACH FORMATTING TO INSERTED CELLS, ROWS, AND COLUMNS

Open the **Insert Options** Smart tag (the paint brush icon that appears after an insert) and choose from which direction you want the formatting applied, or choose to clear formatting.

REMOVING CELLS, ROWS, AND COLUMNS

1. Select the single or adjacent items (cells, rows, or columns) you wish to remove. If you want to remove non-adjacent items, press and hold **CTRL** while clicking them.

2. Open **Edit** and click **Delete**, or right-click the selected items and click **Delete**.

3. In the Delete dialog box, choose from which direction to fill in the removed cells or choose to remove the entire the row or column the items were in.

- To insert graphics or drawing objects, see Chapter 7 for information on working with graphics.

When a selected object changes size or a new object is inserted, if its height becomes larger than the original row height, the height of all cells in the row(s) will be increased. The size of the other cells contents, however, stays the same.

CHANGE ROW HEIGHT TO FIT SIZE OF CELL CONTENTS

Double-click the bottom border of the row header for a row or selected rows.

–Or–

Select the cell or rows you want to size, then open **Format**, point at **Row**, and click **AutoFit**.

The row heights(s) will adjust to fit the highest.

Adjust Column Width

As with changing row height, you can change the width of a column manually or by changing cell contents.

CHANGE THE WIDTH FOR A SINGLE COLUMN

1. Point at the right border of the column header until the pointer changes to a cross with left and right arrowheads.

2. Drag the border to the left or right to the width you want.

E	F	
4th Qtr	**Total Yr**	
$39,876	$137,591	

CHANGE THE WIDTH FOR MULTIPLE COLUMNS

1. Select the columns you want to adjust.

2. Open **Format**, point at **Column**, and click **Width**. The Column Width dialog box opens.

3. Type a new width and click **OK**. The cell width changes, but the size of the cell contents stays the same.

CHANGE COLUMN WIDTH TO FIT SIZE OF CELL CONTENTS

1. Double-click the right border of the column header for the column or selected columns.

   –Or–

   Select the cell or columns you want to size.

2. Open **Format**, point at **Column**, and click **AutoFit Selection**. The column width(s) will adjust to fit the longest entry.

Hide and Unhide Rows and Columns

Hidden rows and columns provide a means to temporarily remove rows or columns from view without deleting them or their contents.

HIDE ROWS AND COLUMNS

1. Select the rows or columns to be hidden. (See the QuickSteps, "Selecting Ranges and Cells" in Chapter 2.)

2. Open **Format**, point at **Row** or **Column**, and click **Hide**; or right-click the selection and choose **Hide**.

   –Or–

   Drag the bottom row border of the rows to be hidden *up*, or drag the right border of the columns to be hidden to the *left*.

The row numbers or column letters of the hidden cells are omitted, as shown in Figure 3-1. (You can also tell cells are hidden by the slightly darker border in the row or column headers between the hidden rows or columns.)

UNHIDE ROWS OR COLUMNS

1. Drag across the row or column headers on either side of the hidden rows or columns.

2. Open **Format**, point at **Row** or **Column**, and click **Unhide**.

   –Or–

   Right-click the selection and choose **Unhide**.

Change Cell Borders

Borders provide a quick and effective way to emphasize and segregate data on a worksheet. You can create borders by choosing from samples, by drawing your own, or by setting them up in a dialog box. Use the method that suits you best.

PICK A BORDER

1. Select the cell, range, row, or column whose border you want modify.

2. On the Formatting toolbar, click the **Borders** down arrow, and select the border style you want. (The style you choose remains as the available border style on the toolbar.)

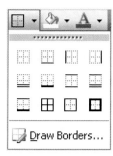

3. To remove a border, select the cell(s), and click the first border style in the first row of choices.

Darker border signifies hidden rows and columns

Figure 3-1: Rows 6 and 7 and column C are hidden in this worksheet

DRAW BORDERS

1. On the Formatting toolbar, click the **Borders** down arrow, and select **Draw Borders**. A Borders toolbar is displayed.

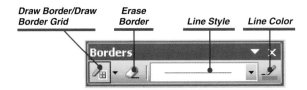

TIP

You can split a cell diagonally with a border by dragging the drawing pointer from opposite corners.

2. Click the **Draw Border/Draw Border Grid** down arrow and choose:

   - **Draw Border**, to draw an outline border on a range of cells

   - **Draw Border Grid**, to add inside borders in a range of cells

3. Select a border style from the Line Style drop-down list and color from the Line Color tool, and then use the drawing pointer to apply the border as you drag. (To remove unwanted borders, drag the **Erase Border** tool over them.) Figure 3-2 shows several border styles.

4. When finished, click the Close button (X) at the top right of the Borders toolbar to return to the standard Excel pointers.

	A	B	C	D	E	F
	Superior Office Supplies					
	2004 Budget					
	Superior Office Supplies	1st Qtr	2nd Qtr	3rd Qtr	4th Qtr	Total Yr
	Revenue					
	Paper Supplies	$23,567	$35,938	$38,210	$39,876	$137,591
	Writing Instruments	$5,437	$5,834	$5,923	$6,082	$23,276
	Cards and Books	$14,986	$15,043	$16,975	$16,983	$63,987
	Other Items	$25,897	$26,729	$27,983	$28,721	$109,330
	Total Revenue	$69,887	$83,544	$89,091	$91,662	$334,184
	Expenses					
	Wages	$8,345	$8,598	$9,104	$9,301	$35,348
	Income tax	$1,252	$1,290	$1,366	$1,395	$5,302
	Social Security	$1,035	$1,066	$1,129	$1,153	$4,383
	Medicare	$242	$249	$264	$270	$1,025

Figure 3-2: Borders can be drawn around the perimeter of a range or applied to the cell perimeters within a range

TIP

You can quickly add solid color and shading to selected cells from the Fill Color button on the Formatting toolbar. Click the button to apply the displayed color, or open a palette by clicking the down arrow next to the button. The last color or shade selected remains on the Fill Color button until changed.

PREVIEW BORDERS BEFORE YOU CHANGE THEM

1. Select the cell, range, row, or column that you want modify with a border.

2. Open **Format**, select **Cells**, and click the **Border** tab. The Format Cells dialog box opens, as shown in Figure 3-3.

3. In the Border area, you will see a preview of the selected cells. Use the other tools in the dialog box to set up your borders.

   - **Presets buttons**, to set broad border parameters by selecting to have no border, an outline border, or an inside "grid" border (can also be changed manually in the Border area)

   - **Line area**, to select a border style and color

   - **Border buttons**, to choose where you want a border (clicked once to add the border, clicked twice to remove it)

4. Click **OK** to apply the borders.

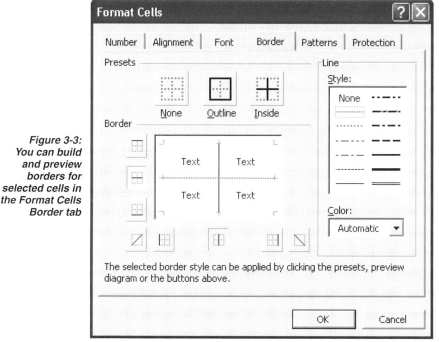

Figure 3-3: You can build and preview borders for selected cells in the Format Cells Border tab

Add a Background

You can add color and shading to selected cells to provide a solid background. You can also add preset patterns alone or in conjunction with a solid background for even more effect.

1. Select the cell, range, row, or column that you want to modify with a background.

2. Open **Format**, select **Cells**, and click the **Patterns** tab. The Format Cells dialog box opens, as shown in Figure 3-4.

3. Select a solid color or grayscale shade.

   –Or–

   Click the **Pattern** down arrow and select one of the preset designs.

   –Or–

   Select both a pattern and a solid background.

4. Preview your selections in the Sample area and click **OK** when finished.

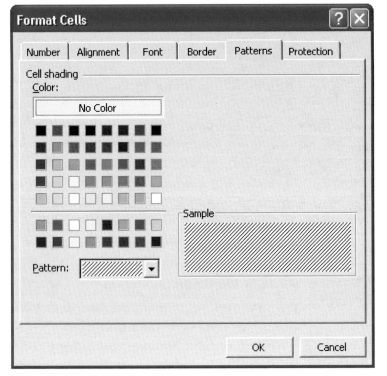

Figure 3-4: Add color, shading, and patterns from the Format Cells dialog box Patterns tab

Add a Comment

A comment acts as a "notepad" for cells, providing a place on the worksheet for explanatory text that's hidden until needed.

1. Select the cell where you want the comment.

2. Open **Insert** and click **Comment**, or right-click the cell and click **Insert Comment**. In either case, a text box labeled with your user name is attached to the cell.

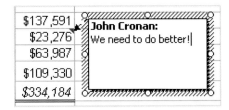

3. Type your comment and click anywhere on the worksheet to close the comment. A red triangle in the upper-right corner of the cell indicates a comment is attached.

Change How Text Looks

Text changes can greatly enhance the appearance of a worksheet. You can change the character appearance with fonts and sizing, change where the text appears in the cell, and apply your changes consistently by setting up styles.

Use Fonts

Each font is comprised of a *typeface*, such as Arial; a *style*, such as Italic; and a size. Other characteristics, such as color and super/subscripting, further distinguish text. Excel also provides several underlining options that are useful in accounting applications.

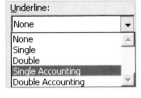

USING COMMENTS

VIEW A COMMENT

Point at or select a cell that displays a red triangle in its upper-right corner. The comment stays displayed as long as your cursor remains in the cell.

–Or–

To keep the comment displayed while doing other work, right-click the cell and click **Show/Hide Comments** on the context menu. (To hide the comment, right-click the cell and click **Hide Comment**.)

–Or–

To view all comments in a worksheet, open **View** and click **Comments.**

EDIT A COMMENT

1. Select a cell that displays a red triangle in its upper-right corner.

2. Open **Insert** and click **Edit Comment**, or right-click the cell and click **Edit Comment** on the context menu.

3. Edit the text, including the user name if appropriate. Click the worksheet when finished.

DELETE A COMMENT

1. Select the cell or cells that contain the comments.

2. Open **Edit**, point at **Clear**, and click **Comments**, or right-click the cell and click **Delete Comments**.

REPOSITION/RESIZE A COMMENT

Open the comment. (See "Edit a Comment.")

- To **Resize**, point at one of the corner or mid-border sizing handles. When the pointer becomes a double arrow-headed line, drag the handle in the direction you want to increase or decrease the comment's size.

Continued...

1. On a worksheet select:

   - **Cells**, to apply font changes to all characters

   - **Characters**, to apply font changes to just the selected text and numbers

2. Open **Format**, select **Cells**, and click the **Font** tab.

   –Or–

   Right-click the selection, click **Format Cells**, and then click the **Font** tab.

3. The Format Cells dialog box Font tab opens, as shown in Figure 3-5. Make and preview changes, and click **OK** when finished.

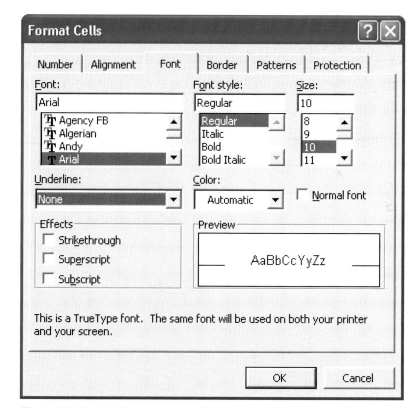

Figure 3-5: Change the appearance of text by changing its font and other characteristics in the Format Cells dialog box Font tab

* To **Move**, point at the wide border surrounding the comment. When the pointer becomes a cross with arrowhead tips, drag the comment to where you want it.

* To **Reposition with cells**, select the comment by clicking the wide border to change it from hashed to dotted. Open **Format**, select **Comment**, and click the **Properties** tab. Select the behavior you want from the three alternatives.

COPY A COMMENT

1. Select the cell that contains the comment you want to copy.

2. Click **Copy** on the Standard toolbar.

   –Or–

   Right-click the cell and click **Copy**.

   –Or–

   Press **CTRL+C**.

3. The cell is surrounded by a flashing border.

4. Open **Edit** and click **Paste Special**. Under Paste, click **Comments**, and then click **OK**.

5. Repeat Step 2 to paste the comment into other cells, or press **ESC** to remove the flashing border.

CHANGE THE APPEARANCE OF COMMENT TEXT

1. To change formatting of existing text, select the text first. If you do not select existing text only new text you type will show the changes after you make them.

2. Right-click the cell with the comment and click **Edit Comment**.

Continued...

NOTE

You cannot cut only the comment to move it. To move the comment you must move the entire cell.

Change Alignment and Orientation

You can modify how characters appear within a cell by changing their alignment, orientation, and "compactness."

1. Select the cells whose contents you want to change.

2. Open **Format**, select **Cells**, and click the **Alignment** tab.

   –Or–

   Right-click the selection, click **Format Cells**, and then click the **Alignment** tab.

3. The Format Cells dialog box Alignment tab opens, as shown in Figure 3-6.

   The specific features of the Alignment tab are described in Table 3-1(see right).

4. Click **OK** when you are finished.

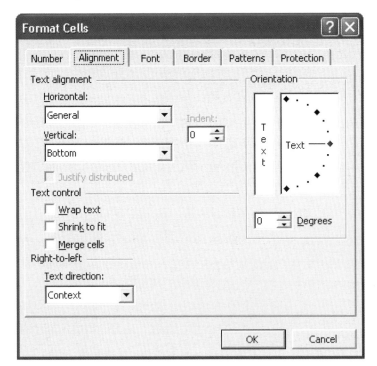

Figure 3-6: Alignment, orientation, and "compactness" of cell contents are modified in the Format Cells dialog box Alignment tab

USING COMMENTS *(Continued)*

3. Double-click the comment border to open the Format Comment dialog box and click the **Font** tab. Make and preview the changes you want, and click **OK**.

CHANGE AN EXISTING COMMENT'S COLOR

1. Right-click the comment, choose **Show/Hide Comment**, and click the comment's wide border to change it from hashed to dotted.

> John Cronan:
> We need to do better!

2. On the Formatting toolbar, click the **Fill Color** down arrow to open the palette. Click the new color you want.

CHANGE NEW COMMENTS' COLOR

1. To change the default color for new comments (and all tooltips, such as button names), right-click the **Windows Desktop**, and select **Properties**. The Display Properties dialog box opens.

2. Click the **Appearance** tab and then click **Advanced**. In the Advanced Appearance dialog box, open the **Item** drop-down list and click **Tooltip**.

3. Click the **Color 1** down arrow to open the palette and select a color. Click **OK** when finished.

CHANGE A COMMENT'S BORDER

1. Right-click the comment, choose **Edit Comment**, and click the wide border to change it from hashed to dotted.

2. Double-click the comment border to open the Format Comment dialog box, and then click the **Colors And Lines** tab. In the Line area, make color, style, thickness changes. Click **OK** when finished.

TABLE 3-1: *The Alignment Tab Offers Several Cell Formatting Options*

FEATURE	OPTION	DESCRIPTION
Text Alignment, Horizontal	General	Right aligns numbers, left aligns text, and centers error values; Excel default setting
	Left (Indent)	Left aligns characters with optional indentation spinner
	Center	Centers characters in the cell
	Right (Indent)	Right aligns characters with optional indentation spinner
	Fill	Fills cell with recurrences of content
	Justify	Justifies the text in a cell so that, to the degree possible, both the left and right ends are vertically aligned.
	Center Across Selection	Centers text across one or more cells; used to center titles across several columns
	Distributed (Indent)	Stretches cell contents across cell width by adding space between words, with optional indentation spinner
	Justify Distributed	Evenly distributes text within the cell, while still meeting the other parameters
Text Alignment Vertical	Top	Places the text at the top of the cell
	Center	Places the text in the center of the cell
	Bottom	Places the text at the bottom of the cell; Excel's default setting
	Justify	Evenly distributes text between the top and bottom of a cell to fill it by adding space between lines
	Distributed	Vertically arranges characters equally within the cell (behaves the same as Justify)
Orientation		Angles text in a cell by dragging the red diamond up or down, or by using the Degrees spinner
Text Control	Wrap Text	Moves text that extends beyond the cell's width to the line below
	Shrink To Fit	Reduces character size so cell contents fit within cell width (cannot be used with Wrap Text)
	Merge Cells	Creates one cell from contiguous cells, "increasing" the width of a cell without changing the width of the column(s)
Right-To-Left, Text Direction		Text entry flows from the right as in many Middle Eastern and East Asian countries

TIP

Several text formatting features available from the Format Cells dialog box are also available on the Formatting toolbar.

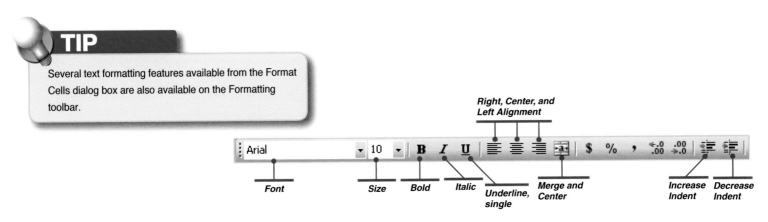

Use Styles

You can apply several cell formatting parameters at one time by creating a *style* that combines them under one name.

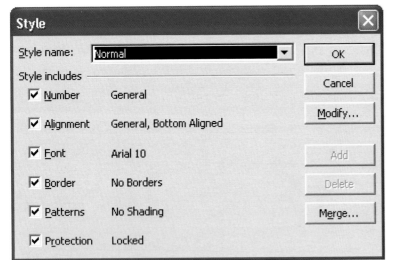

Figure 3-7: Combine several formatting settings into a single style for easy application in the Style dialog box

CREATE A STYLE

1. Open **Format** and click **Style**. The Style dialog box opens, as shown in Figure 3-7.

2. Click **Modify**. Use the Format Cells dialog box to set up the formatting settings you want. Click **OK** when finished.

3. In the Style dialog box, type a name in the **Style Name** text box. Click **Add** and then click **OK**.

APPLY A STYLE

1. Select the cells you want to format with a style.

2. Open **Format** and select **Style**.

3. Click the **Style Name** down arrow to open its drop-down list box, and select the style.

4. Click **OK**. The style's formatting settings will be applied to the selected cells.

ADD STYLES FROM OTHER WORKBOOKS

1. Open both the workbook whose styles you want to add and the workbook where you want the styles to be added.

2. Open **Window** and click the workbook to which you want the styles added, making it the active workbook.

3. Open **Format**, select **Style**, and click **Merge**. In the Merge Style dialog box, click the workbook from which you want to add styles. Click **OK**.

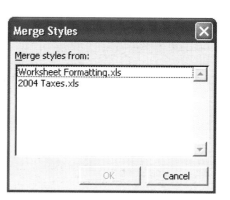

Transfer Formatting

The Format Painter lets you apply formatting from one cell to other cells.

1. Select the cell whose formatting you want to transfer.

2. Point at the **Format Painter icon** on the Standard toolbar, then: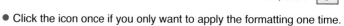

   - Click the icon once if you only want to apply the formatting one time.

     –Or–

   - Double-click the icon to keep the Format Painter turned on for repeated use.

3. Select the cells where you want the formatting applied.

   If you single-clicked the Format Painter before applying it to your selection, it will turn off after applying it to your first selection; if you double-clicked the button, you may select other cells to continue transferring the formatting.

4. Double-click the **Format Painter** button to turn it off.

Format Automatically

Excel provides 16 ready-made formats you can apply in their entirety or apply after you have selectively removed unwanted aspects of the formatting.

1. Select the cells you want to format.

2. Open **Format** and click **AutoFormat**. The AutoFormat dialog box opens, as shown in Figure 3-8.

3. Scroll through the list of formats until you find one close to what you want.

4. Click **Options** and then deselect any formats you want removed.

5. Click **OK** when you are finished.

Figure 3-8:
Choose from
16 ready-made
formats to quickly
enhance your
worksheet

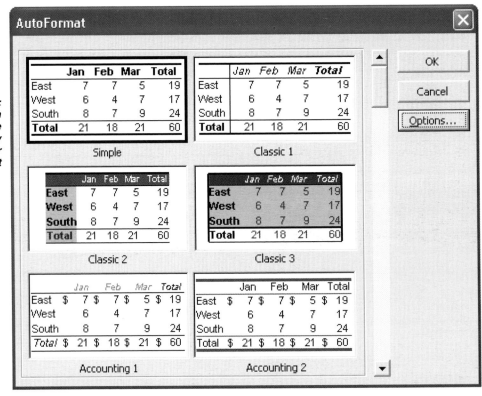

Format Conditionally

Formatting can be applied to a cell based on whether the value of the cell satisfies one or more conditions you set.

1. Select the cells that will be formatted if they meet conditions you set.

2. Open **Format** and click **Conditional Formatting**. The Conditional Formatting dialog box opens, as shown in Figure 3-9.

3. In the Condition 1 area, keep Cell Value in the first drop-down list box (the other choice, "Formula Is," is covered in Chapter 4). Open the second drop-down list box and select the condition. Depending on your condition, you will see one or two value text boxes.

4. Click the first value text box to place the insertion point there and type a constant value.

   –Or–

   Click a cell on the worksheet whose value you want. Its address will be placed in the value text box.

5. Repeat Step 4 for the second value text box, if displayed.

6. Click **Format** to open a modified Format Cells dialog box. Make your formatting choices and click **OK**.

7. In the Conditional Formatting dialog box, click **Add** to include additional conditions or click **OK** to finish.

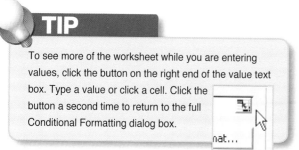

TIP

To see more of the worksheet while you are entering values, click the button on the right end of the value text box. Type a value or click a cell. Click the button a second time to return to the full Conditional Formatting dialog box.

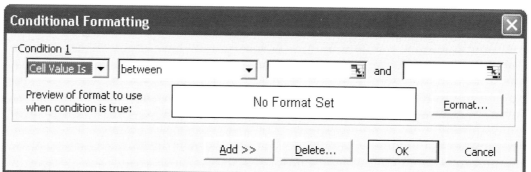

Figure 3-9:
You can format cells
based on one or more
conditions you set

Arrange and Organize Worksheets

Lock Rows and Columns

You can lock rows and columns in place so that they remain visible as you scroll. Typically, row and column headings are locked in larger worksheets.

LOCK ROWS

1. Select the row below the rows you want to lock.

2. Open **Window** and select **Freeze Panes**. A thin border displays on the bottom of the locked row. All rows above the locked row remain in place as you scroll down.

	A	B	C	D	E	F
1	Superior Office Supplies					
2	2004 Budget					
9	Total Revenue	$69,887	$83,544	$89,091	$91,662	$334,184
10						

LOCK COLUMNS

1. Select the column to the right of the columns you want to lock.

2. Open **Window** and select **Freeze Panes**. A thin border displays on the right side of the locked column. All columns to the left of the locked column remain in place as you scroll to the right.

LOCK ROWS AND COLUMNS TOGETHER

1. Select the cell that is below and to the right of the range you want to lock.

2. Open **Window** and select **Freeze Panes**. A thin border displays below the locked rows and to the right of the locked columns. The range will remain in place as you scroll down or to the right.

UNLOCK ROWS AND COLUMNS

Open **Window** and click **Unfreeze Panes**.

NOTE

Freezing panes is not the same as freezing data. In an external data range, you can prevent the data from being refreshed, thereby freezing it. See Chapter 8 for more information on external data ranges.

Split a Worksheet

You can divide a worksheet into two independent panes of the same data, as shown in Figure 3-10.

1. Open **Window** and select **Split**. Horizontal and vertical split bars are displayed across the worksheet. Remove the unwanted split bar by double-clicking it, leaving you with two panes.

2. Point at the split bar and drag the bar up or down, and/or left or right to proportion the two panes as you want.

3. Use the scroll bars to view more data within each pane. You may remove the split bar by double-clicking it.

View Worksheets from Multiple Workbooks

You can divide the Excel worksheet area to view worksheets from multiple workbooks. This arrangement makes it easy to copy data, formulas, and formatting among several worksheets. (See Chapter 9 for information on sharing data.)

1. Open the workbooks that contain the worksheets you want to view. (See Chapter 1 for information on opening existing workbooks.)

2. Open **Window** and click **Arrange**. The Arrange Windows dialog box opens.

3. Select an arrangement and click **OK**. (Figure 3-11 shows an example of tiling three workbooks.)

Figure 3-10: A split worksheet provides two independent views of the same worksheet

The worksheet shows two panes:

Left pane: Superior Office Supplies — 2004 Budget

Superior Office Supplies	1st Qtr	2nd Qtr	3rd Qtr	4th Qtr	Total Yr
Revenue					
Paper Supplies	$23,567	$35,938	$38,210	$39,876	$137,591
Writing Instruments	$5,437	$5,834	$5,923	$6,082	$23,276
Cards and Books	$14,986	$15,043	$16,975	$16,983	$63,987
Other Items	$25,897	$26,729	$27,983	$28,721	$109,330
Total Revenue	$69,887	$83,544	$89,091	$91,662	$334,184
Expenses					
Wages	$8,345	$8,598	$9,104	$9,301	$35,348
Income tax	$1,252	$1,290	$1,366	$1,395	$5,302
Social Security	$1,035	$1,066	$1,129	$1,153	$4,383
Medicare	$242	$249	$264	$270	$1,025

Right pane: Acme Temporary Agency — 2003 Contractors

ID #	Last Name	Position	Company	Start Date	End D
6789	Cronan	warehouse	Superior Office	6-Feb	3-I
5893	Matthews	accounting	ABC	2-Jun	3-
5467	O'Neil	office mgr	WA State	5-Mar	11
6547	Diamanti	warehouse	ABC	6-Aug	8-
7658	Canby	accounting	General	7-May	6-
4587	Curtis	driver	XYZ	4-Oct	5-
3456	Matthews				

Sheet1 / Sheet2 \ Sheet3 /

Ready   NUM

UICKSTEPS

WORKING WITH WORKSHEETS

ADD A WORKSHEET

1. Select the worksheet tab to the right of where you want the new worksheet.

2. Open **Insert** and click **Worksheet**.

DELETE A WORKSHEET

Right-click the worksheet tab of the worksheet you want to delete and click **Delete**.

MOVE OR COPY A WORKSHEET

1. Click the worksheet tab of the worksheet you want to move or copy.

2. In the Move Or Copy dialog box, select the workbook and where you want the worksheet placed.

3. To move the worksheet, click **OK**; to copy the worksheet click **Create A Copy** and then click **OK**.

RENAME A WORKSHEET

1. Right-click the worksheet tab of the worksheet you want to rename and click **Rename**.

2. Type a new worksheet name and press **ENTER**.

COLOR A WORKSHEET TAB

1. Right-click the worksheet tab of the worksheet you want to color and click **Tab Color**.

2. In the Format Tab Color dialog box, select a color from the palette and then click **OK**.

CHANGE THE DEFAULT NUMBER OF WORKSHEETS IN A WORKBOOK

1. Open **Tools**, select **Options**, and click **General**.

2. Use the spinner next to Sheets In New Workbook to change the number of worksheets you want.

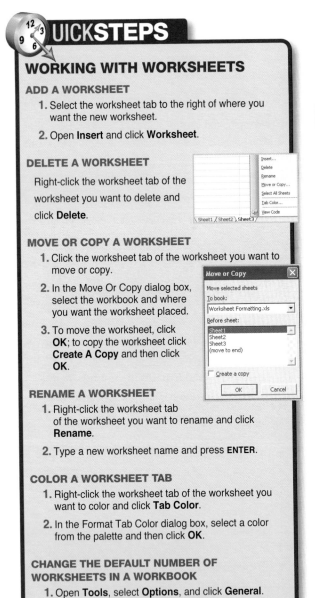

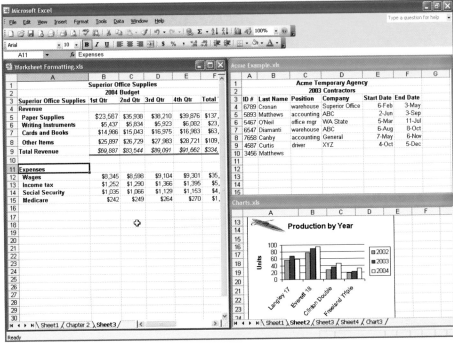

Figure 3-11: You have access to several worksheets when you arrange open workbooks

Chapter 4

Using Formulas and Functions

Excel lets you easily perform powerful calculations using formulas and functions. Formulas are mathematical statements that follow a set of rules and use a specific syntax. In this chapter you will learn how to reference cells used in formulas, to give cells names so they are easily input, and to build formulas. You will also learn about several tools Excel provides to find and correct errors in formulas. Functions are ready-made formulas that you can use to get quick results for specific applications, such as figuring out loan payments.

Reference Cells

Formulas typically make use of data already entered in worksheets and need a scheme to locate, or *reference,* that data. Shortcuts are used to help you recall addresses as well as a *syntax*, or set of rules, to communicate to Excel how you want cells used.

Change Cell References in Formulas

There are three basic methods and one extended method for referencing cells used in formulas that adhere to the Excel default "A1" cell reference scheme used in this book.

TIP

Absolute cell references are typically used when you want to copy the values of cells and are not interested in applying their formulas to other cells, such as in a summary or report where the relative references would be meaningless. Though you can apply absolute reference syntax to each cell reference, a faster way is to open the Paste Smart tag that displays next to the destination cells and choose **Values Only** from the drop-down list.

See "Copy Formulas" later in the chapter for more information on copying and pasting formulas.

334184	
	○ Keep Source Formatting
	○ Match Destination Formatting
	◉ Values Only

- **Relative references** in formulas move with cells as cells are copied or moved around a worksheet. This is the most flexible and common way to use cell references and is the Excel default, displayed as A1 in the worksheet and Formula bar. For example, if you sum a list of quarterly expenses for the first quarter, =SUM(B12:B15), and then copy and paste that summary cell to the summary cells for the other three quarters, Excel will deduce that you want the totals for the other quarters to be =SUM(C12:C15), =SUM(D12:D15), and =SUM(E12:E15). Figure 4-1 shows how this appears on the worksheet.

- **Absolute references** do not change cell addresses when you copy or move formulas. Absolute references are displayed in the worksheet and Formula bar with the dollar sign preceding the reference, for example A1.

- **Mixed references** include one relative and one absolute cell reference. Such references are displayed in the worksheet and Formula bar with a dollar sign preceding the absolute reference but no dollar sign before the relative reference. For example, $A1 indicates absolute column, relative row; A$1 indicates relative column, absolute row.

- **External (or 3D) references** are an extended form of relative, absolute, and mixed cell references. They are used when referencing cells from other worksheets or workbooks. Such a reference might look like this in the worksheet and Formula bar: [*workbook name*]*worksheet name*!A1.

To change cell referencing:

1. Select the cell that contains the formula reference you want to change.

2. In the Formula bar, select the cell address and press **F4** to switch the cell referencing, starting from a relative reference to the following in this order:

   - Absolute (A1)

   - Mixed (relative column, absolute row) (A$1)

   - Mixed (absolute column, relative row) ($A1)

- Relative (A1)

  –Or–

- Edit the cell address by entering or removing the dollar symbol ($) in front of row or column identifiers.

Figure 4-1: Using relative references, Excel logically assumes which cells to sum when copying B16 to C16, D16, and E16

Copying B16, which sums B12 through B15,...

B16	▼	fx	=SUM(B12:B15)		
	A	B	C	D	E
1		Superior Office Supplies			
2		2004 Budget			
3	Superior Office Supplies	1st Qtr	2nd Qtr	3rd Qtr	4th Qtr
11	Expenses				
12	Wages	8345	8598	9104	9301
13	Income tax	=B12*0.15	=C12*0.15	=D12*0.15	=E12*0.15
14	Social Security	=B12*0.124	=C12*0.124	=D12*0.124	=E12*0.124
15	Medicare	=B12*0.029	=C12*0.029	=D12*0.029	=E12*0.029
16	Total	=SUM(B12:B15)	=SUM(C12:C15)	=SUM(D12:D15)	=SUM(E12:E15)
17					

... and pasting into C16, D16, and E16 provides correct cell addresses for column totals

TIP

Press CTRL+` to view formulas instead of cell values, as shown in Figure 4-1. The ` character is the grave accent found on the upper-left of the keyboard on the same key as the tilde (~). Press the key combination a second time to return to a value display.

Change to R1C1 References

You can change the A1 cell referencing scheme used by Excel to an older style that identifies both rows and columns numerically starting in the upper-left corner of the worksheet, rows first, and adds a leading *R* and *C* for clarification. For example, cell B4 in R1C1reference style is R4C2.

1. Open **Tools**, select **Options**, and click the **General** tab.

2. Under Settings, click **R1C1 Reference Style**.

Settings

☐ R1C1 reference style

USING CELL REFERENCE OPERATORS

Cell reference operators (colons, commas, and spaces used in an address such as E5:E10 E16:E17,E12) provide the syntax for referencing cell ranges, unions, and intersections.

REFERENCE A RANGE

A *range* defines a block of cells.

Type a colon (:) between the upper-leftmost cell and the lower-rightmost cell (for example, B5:C8).

=SUM(B5:C8)

B	C
$23,567	$35,938
$5,437	$5,834
$14,986	$15,043
$25,897	$26,729

REFERENCE A UNION

A *union* joins multiple cell references.

Type a comma (,) between separate cell references (for example B5,B7,C6).

=SUM(B5,B7,C6)

B	C
$23,567	$35,938
$5,437	$5,834
$14,986	$15,043

REFERENCE AN INTERSECTION

An *intersection* is the overlapping, or common cells in two ranges.

Type a space (**SPACEBAR**) between two range-cell references (for example B5:B8 B7:C7). B7 is the common cell.

B5:B8 B7:C7)

B	C
$23,567	$35,938
$5,437	$5,834
$14,986	$15,043
$25,897	$26,729

NOTE

You can also name a range of cells; however, you may use a named range only with Excel's built-in functions. If you try to use a named range within a formula you create, Excel will return an error. (See "Use Functions" later in this chapter.)

Name a Cell

You can name a cell (MonthTotal, for example) instead of referring to its physical cell address and then use the name when referencing the cell in formulas and functions. Names are more descriptive, easier to remember, and often quicker to enter than A1-style cell references.

1. Select the cell you want to reference.
2. Click the **Name** box on the left of the Formula bar.
3. Type a name (no spaces allowed), and press **ENTER**.

MonthTotal ▼		fx =SUM(B5:B8)	
A	B	C	D

Go to a Named Cell

Named cells are quickly found and selected for you.

- Click the down arrow on the right end of the Name box to open the drop-down list and click the named cell you want to go to.

  –Or–

- Open **Edit**, and click **Go To** (you may have to extend the menu). The Go To dialog box opens. Double-click the named cell you want to go to.

Go To

Go to:

constant
QtrExpenses
QtrTotals
TotRevenue

Build Formulas

Formulas are mathematical equations that combine *values* and *cell references* with *operators* to calculate a result. Values are the contents of cells, including numbers and logical values such as True and False. Cell references point to cells whose values are to be used, for example E5:E10, E12, and MonthlyTot. Operators, such as + (add), > (greater than), and ^ (use an exponent), tell Excel what type of calculation to perform or logical comparison to apply. Prebuilt formulas, or *functions*, that return a value also can be used in formulas. (Functions are described later in this chapter.)

Create a Formula

You create formulas by either entering or referencing values. The character that tells Excel to perform a calculation is the equal sign (=) and must precede any combination of values, cell references, and operators.

Excel formulas are calculated from left to right, according to an ordered hierarchy of operators. For example, exponents precede multiplication and division, which precede addition and subtraction. You can alter the calculation order (and results) by use of parentheses; Excel performs the calculation within the innermost parentheses first. For example, =12+48/24 returns 14 (48 is divided by 24, resulting in 2; then 12 is added to 2). Using parentheses, =(12+48)/24 returns 2.5 (12 is added to 48, resulting in 60; then 60 is divided by 24).

TIP

Excel provides several concessions for users who are transitioning to Excel from Lotus 1-2-3. When creating a formula, you can type a plus sign (+) instead of the equal sign to denote a formula. Excel will change the plus sign to an equal sign if a number follows it, or Excel will add the equal sign to a plus sign that is followed by a cell reference. In any case, be sure not to type a leading space before either the plus or the equal sign, as the characters that follow will be interpreted as text instead of as a formula.

ENTER A SIMPLE FORMULA

1. Select a blank cell, and type an equal sign (=). The equal sign displays in the cell and in the Formula bar.

2. Type a value, such as 64.

3. Type an operator, such as +.

4. Type a second value, such as 96.

5. Complete the entry by pressing **ENTER,** or add additional values and operators and then complete the entry. The result of your equation displays in the cell. (See Chapter 2 for other methods to complete an entry.)

CAUTION

When creating a formula, be careful not to click any cells that you do not want referenced in the formula. After you type the equal sign, Excel interprets any selected cell as being a cell reference in the formula.

USE CELL REFERENCES

1. Select a blank cell, and type an equal sign (=). The equal sign displays in the cell and in the Formula bar.

2. Enter a cell reference:

   - Type a cell reference (for example, B4) that contains the value you want.

   - Click the cell whose value you want. A blinking border surrounds the cell.

   - Select a named cell. Open **Insert**, point at **Name**, and click **Paste**. In the Paste Name dialog box, double-click the named cell.

3. Type an operator.

4. Enter another cell reference or a value.

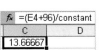

5. Complete the entry by pressing **ENTER**, or add additional cell references, values, and operators and then complete the entry. The result of your equation displays in the cell.

Edit a Formula

You can easily change a formula after you have entered one.

1. Double-click the cell that contains the formula you want to change. The formula is displayed in the cell and in the Formula bar. Cell references for each cell or range are color-coded.

2. Edit the formula by:

   - Making changes directly in the cell or on the Formula bar

   - Dragging the border of a colored cell or range reference to move it to a new location

   - Dragging a corner sizing-box of a colored cell or range reference to expand the reference

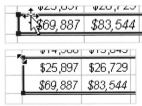

3. Complete the entry by pressing **ENTER**.

Move Formulas

You move formulas by cutting and pasting. When you move formulas, Excel uses absolute referencing. (See "Change Cell References in Formulas" earlier in the chapter for more information on cell referencing.)

1. Right-click the cell whose formula you want to move, and click **Cut**; or select the cell and press **CTRL+X**.

2. Right-click the cell where you want to move the formula, and click **Paste**; or select the new cell, and press **CTRL+V**.

Copy Formulas

When you copy formulas, relative referencing is applied. Therefore, cell referencing in a formula will change when you copy the formula unless you have made a reference absolute. If you do not get the results you expect, click **Undo**, and change the cell references before you copy again.

COPY FORMULAS INTO ADJACENT CELLS

1. Select the cell whose formula you want to copy.

2. Point at the fill handle in the lower-right corner of the cell, and drag over the cells where you want the formula copied.

COPY FORMULAS INTO NONADJACENT CELLS

1. Select the cell whose formula you want to copy, and click **Copy**; or select the cell, and press **CTRL+C**.

2. Do one of these:

   • Copy formatting along with the formula by right-clicking the new cell and clicking **Paste**, or selecting the new cell and pressing **CTRL+V**.

   –Or–

   • Copy just the formula by opening **Edit** and clicking **Paste Special**. In the Paste Special dialog box, click **Formulas**, and then click **OK**.

NOTE

After you have moved the cell, the formula remains exactly the same as it was originally, with the same cell references. That is what I mean by "When you move formulas, Excel uses absolute referencing."

Recalculate Formulas

By default, Excel automatically recalculates formulas affected by changes to a value, to the formula itself, or to a changed named cell. You also can recalculate more frequently using Table 4-1:

TABLE 4-1: *You can recalculate formulas according to several criteria*

TO CALCULATE...	IN...	PRESS...
Formulas, and formulas dependent on them, that have changed since the last calculation	All open workbooks	F9
Formulas, and formulas dependent on them, that have changed since the last calculation	The active worksheet	SHIFT+F9
All formulas regardless of any changes since the last calculation	All open workbooks	CTRL+ALT+F9
All formulas regardless of any changes since the last calculation, after rechecking dependent formulas	All open workbooks	CTRL+SHIFT+ALT+F9

To turn off automatic calculation and set other calculation options:

1. Open **Tools**, select **Options**, and click the **Calculation** tab.

2. In the Calculation area, click the option you want. You can also force an immediate calculation by clicking **Calc Now** or **Calc Sheet**. Click **OK** when finished.

Use External References in Formulas

You can *link* data using cell references to worksheets and workbooks other than the one you are currently working in. For example, if you are building a departmental budget, you could link to each division's budget workbook and have any changes made to formulas in those workbooks automatically applied to your total budget workbook. Changes made to the *external* references in the *source* workbooks are automatically updated in the *destination* workbook when the destination workbook is opened or when the source workbooks are changed and the destination workbook is open.

CREATE EXTERNAL REFERENCE LINKS

1. Open both the source and destination workbooks in your computer.

2. Arrange the workbooks so they are all displayed. For example, open **Window**, select **Arrange**, and click **Tiled**. Click **OK**.

3. In the destination worksheet, create the formula or open an existing formula.

4. Place the insertion point in the formula where you want the external reference.

5. In the source workbook, click the cell whose cell reference you want. The external reference is added to the formula.

   $\times \checkmark f_x$ ='Formulas and Functions.xls'!TotRevenue+A3

6. Press **ENTER** to complete the entry.

UPDATE AND MANAGE EXTERNAL REFERENCES

You can control how external references are updated, check on their status, and break or change the link.

1. Open the destination workbook.

2. Open **Edit** and click **Links**. The Edit Links dialog box opens, as shown in Figure 4-2.

3. Select a link, and then use the command buttons on the right side of the dialog box to perform the action you want.

4. Click **Close** when finished.

Figure 4-2: Update and manage links in the Edit Links dialog box

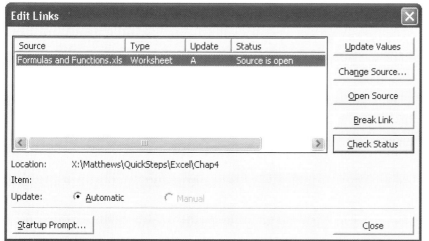

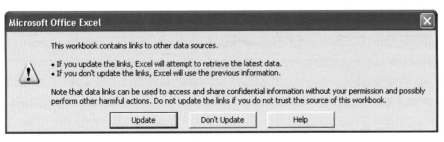

Microsoft Office Excel

This workbook contains links to other data sources.

- If you update the links, Excel will attempt to retrieve the latest data.
- If you don't update the links, Excel will use the previous information.

Note that data links can be used to access and share confidential information without your permission and possibly perform other harmful actions. Do not update the links if you do not trust the source of this workbook.

[Update]　[Don't Update]　[Help]

Figure 4-3: You can allow users the option of updating external references (or links) by displaying this dialog box

CHANGE HOW LINKS ARE UPDATED

When you open a workbook with external links, you can choose whether to update the external links automatically (when the destination workbook is open and the source workbooks are closed) or whether to display an update message box, shown in Figure 4-3, that lets users update the external links.

1. Open **Edit**, select **Links**, and click the **Startup Prompt** button. The Startup Prompt dialog box opens.

2. Select the update option you want, and click **OK**.

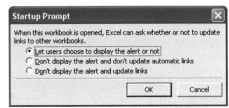

Startup Prompt

When this workbook is opened, Excel can ask whether or not to update links to other workbooks.

- Let users choose to display the alert or not
- Don't display the alert and don't update automatic links
- Don't display the alert and update links

[OK]　[Cancel]

Use Functions

Functions are prewritten formulas that you can use to perform specific tasks. They can be as simple as =PI(), which returns 3.14159265358979, the value of the constant pi; or they can be as complex as =PPMT(rate,per,nper,pv,fv,type), which returns a payment on an investment principal.

A function is comprised of three components.

- **Formula identifier**, the equal sign (=), is required when a function is at the beginning of the formula.

- **Function name** identifies the function and typically is a two- to five-character upper-case abbreviation.

- **Arguments** are the values acted upon by functions to derive a result. They can be numbers, cell references, constants, logical (True or False) values, or a formula. Arguments are separated by commas and enclosed in parentheses.

Enter a Function

You can enter functions on a worksheet by typing or by a combination of typing and selecting cell references, as described earlier in this chapter for formulas. Additionally, you can search for and choose functions from Excel's library of built-in functions.

TIP

You do not need to type the closing parenthesis; Excel will add it for you when you complete the entry. However, it is good practice to include a closing parenthesis for each opening parenthesis. This is especially true if you use complex, *nested* functions that include other functions as arguments. (You may nest up to seven levels!)

TYPE A FUNCTION

To type a function in a cell on the worksheet:

1. Select a blank cell, and type an equal sign (=). The equal sign displays in the cell and the Formula bar.

2. Type the function name, such as AVERAGE, MAX, or PMT.

3. Type an opening parenthesis. Excel displays a ScreenTip showing arguments and proper syntax for the function.

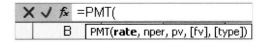

4. Depending on the function, for each argument you need to do none, one, or both of the following:

   ● Type the argument.

   ● Select a cell reference.

5. Type a comma to separate arguments, and repeat Step 4 as necessary.

6. Type a closing parenthesis, and press **ENTER** or click **Enter** on the Formula bar to complete the entry. A value will be returned. (If a *#code* is displayed in the cell or a message box displays indicating you made an error, see "Find and Correct Errors" later in this chapter.)

INSERT A FUNCTION

1. Select a blank cell, open **Insert**, and click **Function**; or click **Insert Function** on the Formula bar. The Insert Function dialog box opens, as shown in Figure 4-4.

Figure 4-4: You can search for and select functions from Excel's extensive library in the Insert Function dialog box

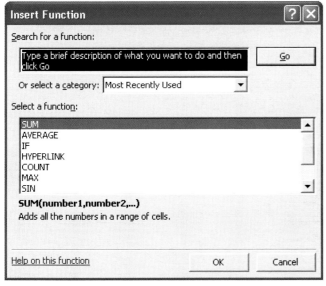

NOTE

You can create your own functions using Excel's built-in programming language, VBA (Visual Basic for Applications).

2. Do one of the following:

- Type a brief description of what you want to do in the **Search For A Function** text box, and click **Go**. A list of recommended functions is displayed in the Select A Function list box.

    –Or–

- Open the **Select A Category** drop-down list, and select a category.

3. Click the function you want from the **Select A Function** list box. Its arguments and syntax are shown, as well as a description of what the function returns.

4. If you need more assistance with the function, click **Help On This Function**. A Help topic provides details on the function and an example of how it's used.

5. Click **OK** to open the Function Arguments dialog box, shown in Figure 4-5. The function's arguments are listed in order at the top of the dialog box, and the beginning of the function displays in the cell and in the Formula bar.

6. Enter values for the arguments by typing or clicking cell references. Click the **Collapse Dialog** button to shrink the dialog box so you can see more of the worksheet. The formula on the worksheet is built as you enter each argument.

7. Click **OK** to complete the entry.

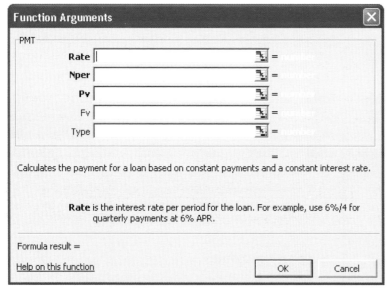

Figure 4-5: Type or click cell references to enter argument values

Sum Numbers in Columns or Rows Quickly

AutoSum uses the SUM function to add contiguous numbers quickly.

1. Select a blank cell below a column or to the right of a row of numbers.
2. Click **AutoSum** on the Standard toolbar. The cells Excel "thinks" you want to sum above or to the left of the blank cell are enclosed in a border, and the formula is displayed in the cell and in the Formula bar.
3. Modify the cells to be included in the sum by dragging a corner sizing-box, editing the formula in the cell or the Formula bar, or by selecting cells.
4. Press **ENTER** or click **Enter** on the Formula bar to complete the entry. The sum of the selected cells is returned.

   –Or–

1. Select a contiguous column or row of cells including a blank cell at the end of the column or to the right of the row.
2. Click **AutoSum**. The sum is entered in the blank cell.

Find and Correct Errors

Excel provides several tools that help you see how your formulas and functions are constructed, recognize errors in formulas, and better locate problems. The error-checking tools are available from the Formula Auditing toolbar. To display the toolbar, open **View**, point at **Toolbars**, and click **Formula Auditing**.

NOTE

You can perform the same actions and access the same dialog boxes from the Smart tag that is displayed next to a selected cell containing an error as you can from the Error Checking button on the Formula Auditing toolbar.

Check for Errors

1. Click **Error Checking** on the Formula Auditing toolbar. If you have an error on the worksheet, the Error Checking dialog box opens, as shown in Figure 4-6.

2. Use the command buttons on the left side of the dialog box to perform the indicated action. Click **Next** or **Previous** to check on other errors.

3. Click **Options** to view the Error Checking tab (same tab as in the Tools menu, Options dialog box) where you can customize error checking:

   - **Settings** lets you turn on or off error checking as you enter formulas and determines the color of flagged cells that contain errors. Errors are flagged in green by default.

20	#NAME?

   - **Rules** provides several criteria that cells are checked against for possible errors.

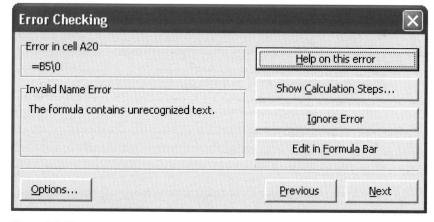

Figure 4-6: You can manage how errors are checked and locate cells that contain errors in the Error Checking dialog box

Trace Precedent and Dependent Cells

Precedent cells are referenced in a formula or function in another cell; that is, they provide a value to a formula or function.

Dependent cells contain a formula or function that uses the value from another cell ; that is, they depend on the value in another cell for their own value.

This interwoven relationship of cells can compound one error into many, making a visual representation of the cell dependencies a vital error correction tool.

1. Click a cell that uses cell references and/or is itself used as a reference by another cell in its formula or function.

2. On the Formula Auditing toolbar, do one or more of the following:

- Click **Trace Precedents** to display blue arrows that point to the cell from other cells.

- Click **Trace Dependents** to display blue arrows that point to other cells.

- Click one of the three removal buttons to remove precedent, dependent, or all arrows.

TIP

To remove a watch you have placed, open the Watch Window by selecting **View**, choosing **Toolbars,** and clicking **Watch Window**. Select the watch you want to remove, and click **Delete Watch**.

Watch a Cell

You can follow what changes are made to a cell's value as its precedent cells' values are changed, even if the cells are not currently visible.

1. Click **Show Watch Window** on the Formula Auditing toolbar; or open **View**, point at **Toolbars**, and click **Watch Window**. The Watch Window toolbar opens.

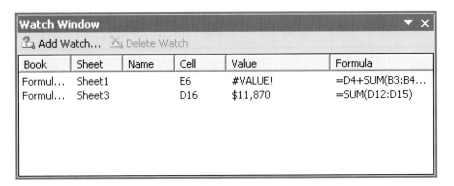

2. Click **Add Watch** to open the Add Watch dialog box.

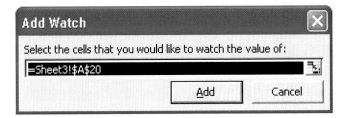

3. Select the cell or cells you want to watch, and click **Add**. Each selected cell will be listed individually in the Watch Window. As changes are made to a precedent cell, the value of the cells "being watched" will be updated according to the recalculation options you have set. (See Recalculate Formulas earlier in the chapter.)

Evaluate a Formula in Pieces

You can see what value will be returned by individual cell references or expressions in the order they are placed in the formula.

1. Select the cell that contains the formula you want to evaluate.

2. Click **Evaluate Formula** on the Formula Auditing toolbar. The Evaluate Formula dialog box, shown in Figure 4-7, opens.

3. Do one or more of the following:

   - Click **Evaluate** to return the value of the first cell reference or expression. The cell reference or expression is underlined.

   - Continue clicking **Evaluate** to return values for each of the cell references or expressions (again, underlined) to the right in the formula. Eventually this will return the value for the cell.

   - Click **Restart** to start the evaluation from the leftmost expression. (The Evaluate button changes to Restart after you have stepped throught the formula.)

   - Click **Step In** to view more data on the underlined cell reference.

   - Click **Step Out** to return to the formula evaluation.

4. Click **Close** when finished.

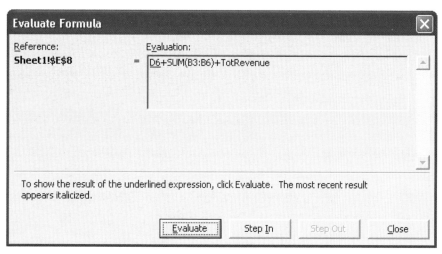

Figure 4-7: You can dissect each expression or component of a formula to see its cell reference, its formula, and its value

Chapter 5
Printing Data

In this chapter you will learn how to print the information you want from a worksheet. Excel provides several tools and options that allow you to add or change printing features before you begin the final stages of printing. Besides making the printed pages easier to read and understand, you can save yourself time by saving the print options for subsequent use. Excel also provides a robust previewing feature so you can review your settings before actually printing.

Set Up the Print Job

You can transform an otherwise nondescript worksheet full of text and numbers into an easy-to-follow, organized report by adding or modifying printing features. You will learn how to add headers and footers, page titles, and other organizational and visual enhancements to your worksheets.

Add Headers and Footers

Custom *headers* and *footers* that print on each page can greatly enhance the appearance of your printed data. Headers and footers, shown in Figure 5-1, are dedicated areas of the printed page—headers at the top and footers at the bottom—where you can place titles, page numbers, dates, and even add pictures.

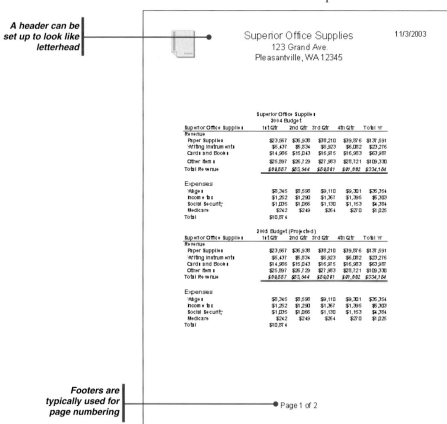

A header can be set up to look like letterhead

Footers are typically used for page numbering

Figure 5-1: A header and footer can enhance the appearance of each page of printed data

CREATE A SIMPLE HEADER AND/OR FOOTER

To select from several common layouts:

1. Open the workbook that contains the data you want to print with a header and/or footer.

2. Open **File**, select **Page Setup**, and click the **Header/Footer** tab. The Header/Footer tab opens as shown in Figure 5-2.

3. Open either the **Header** or **Footer** drop-down list box and select a built-in format. The format displays in the respective preview area.

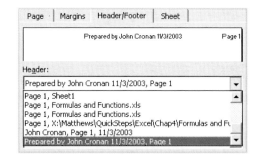

4. Either:

    ● Click **OK** to accept the format.

    –Or–

    ● See the next section, "Customize a Header and Footer."

CUSTOMIZE A HEADER AND FOOTER

1. Open the workbook that contains the data you want to print with a headers and/or footer.

2. Open **File**, select **Page Setup**, and click the **Header/Footer** tab.

3. If you want to start from a built-in format, select one from the **Header** or **Footer** drop-down list boxes.

4. Click either **Custom Header** or **Custom Footer**. A Header or Footer dialog box, identical except for the title, opens as shown in Figure 5-3.

5. Click a text box where you want to add text or objects. The alignment in a text box is the same as the name of its section; for example, the left section is aligned left.

6. Click in the text box where you want the header or footer, and if desired, place the insertion point where you want it within any existing characters. Then do one or more of the following:

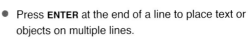

- Type characters.

- Click a button from the row of buttons in the center of the dialog box to add a format. (See the QuickSteps "Formatting Headers and Footers" for information on what the buttons do.)

- Use a combination of typing and features provided by the buttons.

- Press **ENTER** at the end of a line to place text or objects on multiple lines.

7. Click **OK** when finished. The content of your header or footer is shown in the Header/Footer tab.

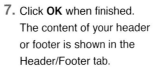

8. Do one of the following:

- Click **OK** a second time to complete the header or footer.

- Click the respective **Custom** button to make a new header or footer.

- Click the respective **Custom** button to change an existing header or footer.

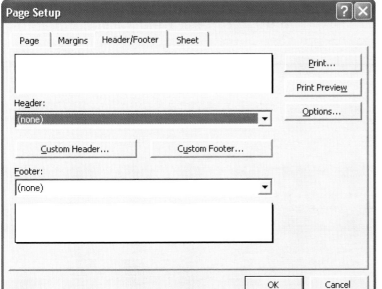

Figure 5-2: The Page Setup Header/Footer dialog box is the gateway to select or create custom headers and footers

QUICKSTEPS

FORMATTING HEADERS AND FOOTERS

Open **File**, select **Page Setup**, choose the **Header/Footer** tab, and click **Custom Header** or **Custom Footer**.

CHANGE CHARACTER FONT, STYLE, AND SIZE

1. Click the **Font** button. The Font dialog box opens. **A**
2. From the list boxes, select the font, font style, size, and other effects you want characters to display.
3. Click **OK**.

INSERT PAGE NUMBERS

To add a page number on every printed page:

1. Click the left, center, or right section you want, positioning the insertion point where you want the page number to appear with other text and spacing.
2. Click the **Page** button.
3. Click **OK**.

INSERT THE TOTAL NUMBER OF PAGES

To add the total number of pages, typically combined with the page number of the page, for example, Page *1 of 2*, as shown at the bottom of Figure 5-1:

1. Click the section you want, positioning the insertion point where you want the total number of pages to appear.
2. Click the **Pages** button.
3. Click **OK**.

INSERT THE PRINT DATE

To add the date the document is printed, in the form mm/dd/yyyy (see Chapter 2):

1. Click the section you want, positioning the insertion point where you want the date to appear.
2. Click the **Date** button.
3. Click **OK**.

Continued...

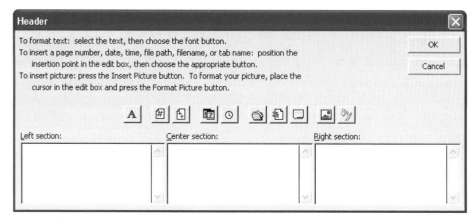

Figure 5-3: The Header and Footer dialog boxes provide identical tools to add formatting and functionality to the top and bottom of all printed pages

Add Pictures to Headers and Footers

To insert pictures such as photos, clip art, and other digital graphic files in the header or footer:

1. Display the Header or Footer dialog box by opening **File**, selecting **Page Setup**, choosing the **Header/Footer** tab, and clicking **Custom Header** or **Custom Footer**.

2. Click the section you want (see Figure 5-3), positioning the insertion point where you want the picture to appear.

3. Click the **Picture** button. In the Insert Picture dialog box, locate the picture you want, and click **OK**.

4. To change the picture's size, orientation, or other formatting, click the **Format Picture** button. Make your changes and click **OK**. (See Chapter 7 for more information on formatting pictures.)

5. Click **OK** in the Header or Footer dialog box.

Adjust Margins

You can adjust the distance between the edges of the printed page and where worksheet text and pictures start printing, and where headers and footer start printing.

To adjust margins, open **File**, select **Page Setup**, and click **Margins**. The Margins tab of the Page Setup dialog box opens, as shown in Figure 5-4.

ADJUST PAGE MARGINS

1. Adjust the **Top**, **Bottom**, **Left** and/or **Right** spinners to change the distance that text and pictures starting printing from the page edges. As you click a spinner, the preview area shows the location of the margin you are working on.
2. Click **OK** when finished making changes in the Page Setup dialog box.

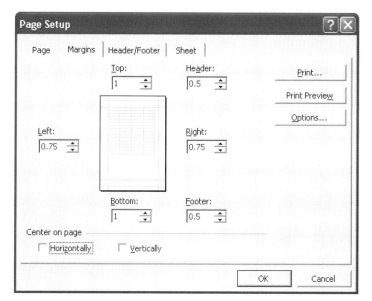

Figure 5-4: Margins for printing worksheet text and objects, and headers and footers, are set in the Margins tab of the Page Setup dialog box

5

CENTER PRINTED DATA BETWEEN MARGINS

Under Center On Page, click one or both:

- **Horizontally,** to print data centered between the Left and Right margins
- **Vertically,** to print data centered between the Top and Bottom margins

ADJUST HEADER AND FOOTER MARGINS

You can change the distance a header starts printing from the top edge of a page, or the distance a footer starts printing from the bottom edge of the page.

1. Adjust the **Header** and/or **Footer** spinners to change the distance that header or footer text and pictures start printing from the top or bottom page edge, respectively.

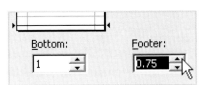

2. Click **OK** when finished making changes in the Page Setup dialog box.

Select Page Orientation and Scaling

Pages can be printed in *portrait*, where a standard 8 ½ x 11 inch piece of paper is printed with the sides being the longer dimension, or in *landscape*, where the top and bottom edges are longer. You can also shrink or enlarge the data displayed in a worksheet, or *scale* it, to get more data to print on a page or focus in on a specific region.

To select a page orientation and/or adjust the scaling, open **File**, select **Page Setup**, and click the **Page** tab.

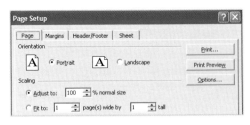

PRINT TALL OR WIDE

1. Under Orientation, select the layout, Portrait (tall) or Landscape (wide), that works best for how your data is arranged in the worksheet.
2. Click **OK**.

SCALE YOUR DATA FOR PRINTING

Under Scaling, either:

- Change the **Adjust To** spinner to increase (see text and objects larger, but fewer cells) or decrease (see text and objects smaller, but more cells) the percentage of magnification.

  –Or–

- Select **Fit To** and change how to arrange the data to be printed by getting more to print across or down a page.

Use Headings as Page Titles

You can use headings as page titles for long lists of horizontal or vertical data so that the headings are printed on every page, keeping you from having to return to the start of the worksheet to see what category of data is being displayed.

1. Open **File**, select **Page Setup**, and click the **Sheet** tab.

2. Under Print Titles, click the **Collapse Dialog** button to the right of:

   - **Rows To Repeat At Top,** to create horizontal titles at the top of every page

     –Or–

   - **Columns To Repeat At Left,** to create vertical titles along the leftmost column of every page

3. Select the rows or columns you want, and click **Close**.

4. Click **OK**.

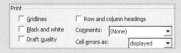

CHOOSING WORKSHEET PRINT OPTIONS

Prior to printing, you can choose several options for including or removing worksheet elements as well as the quality of the print. Open **File**, select **Page Setup**, and click the **Sheet** tab. In the Print area:

PRINT GRIDLINES

To print the lines that outline the worksheet grid of rows, columns, and cells, select **Gridlines**.

PRINT IN BLACK AND WHITE

To save on color ink for draft prints or otherwise print in monochrome, select **Black And White**.

PRINT USING LESS INK OR TONER

Select **Draft Quality.**

PRINT ROW NUMBERS AND COLUMN LETTERS

By default, the row numbers and column letters that define the addressing in a worksheet are not included when a worksheet prints. To include them both, select **Row And Column Headings**.

Change the Order Pages Print

Excel assumes a portrait (tall) page orientation and logically prints down the worksheet as far as there is data. It then moves to the right one page width and prints data down that swath as far as there is data, and so forth. If you choose a landscape (wide) orientation, it will probably make more sense to first print pages across, then down.

1. Open **File**, select **Page Setup**, and click the **Sheet** tab.

2. Under Page Order, select the printing order that works best for the way you have data arranged on the worksheet.

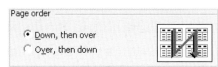

3. Click **OK**.

Print Comments

You can print comments in a list at the end of a worksheet, or you can print them as, and where, they appear on the worksheet. See the QuickSteps "Choosing Worksheet Print Options" for other choices.

1. Open **File**, select **Page Setup**, and click the **Sheet** tab.

2. In the Print area, open the **Comments** drop-down list box and choose where to print the comments.

PRINT COMMENTS IN A LIST

Click **At End Of Sheet** to print comments on a separate page, listed by cell, author, and comment.

PRINT COMMENTS AS DISPLAYED

1. Click **As Displayed On Sheet** to print comments that are shown on the worksheet.

2. To display a comment, right-click the comment and click **Show/Hide Comments**. (See Chapter 3)

QUICKSTEPS

CHOOSING WHAT TO PRINT

You have several options when you decide what portion of a workbook you wanted printed. You can print the entire workbook, selected sheets, an area you define, and selected pages. Most options are available in the Print dialog box. To open the Print dialog box use any of the following:

- Open **File** and click **Print**.

  –Or–

- Press **CTRL+P**.

  –Or–

- Click the **Print** button in the Page Setup dialog box or in Print Preview.

  After choosing what to print, click **OK**.

PRINT A SELECTION

1. Select the cells you want to print.
2. In the Print dialog box, under Print What, click **Selection**.

PRINT SELECTED SHEETS

1. Select sheets to be printed by pressing and holding **CTRL** and clicking the sheet tabs.

Continued...

Print the Data

In this section you will see how to print different segments of a workbook or worksheet, how to preview your settings and make adjustments, and how to change aspects related to the physical device(s) you use to print.

Use Print Areas

You can define a *print area* of a worksheet by selecting one or more ranges of cells that you want to print. Setting this area is especially useful if you print the same selected cells often. The print area is saved along with the other changes to the worksheet when the workbook is saved.

CREATE A PRINT AREA

1. Open **View** and click **Page Break Preview**.

2. Select the range of cells you want in the print area by dragging from the upper-leftmost cell to the lower-rightmost cell.

3. To save this selection:

   - Right-click the selection and click **Set Print Area**.

     –Or–

   - Open **File**, point at **Print Area,** and click **Set Print Area**.

     –Or–

   - Open **File**, select **Page Setup**, and click the **Sheet** tab. In the Print Area text box, type the range to print, or click the **Collapse Dialog** button, select the cells, and click **Close**.

4. Click **OK**.

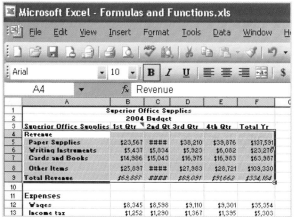

CHOOSING WHAT TO PRINT
(Continued)

2. In the Print dialog box, under Print What, click **Active Sheet(s)**.

–Or–

To print only the active sheet you are looking at, click **Print** on the Standard toolbar.

PRINT ALL SHEETS

In the Print dialog box, under Print What, click **Entire Workbook**.

PRINT SPECIFIC PAGES

1. In the Print dialog box, under Print Range, click **Page(s)**.

2. Do one of the following:

* To print a range of pages, use the **From** and **To** spinners to set the starting and ending pages to print.

  –Or–

* To print one page, set both the **From** and **To** spinners to the same page number.

  –Or–

* To print from a page to the last page, set only the **From** spinner.

PRINT A PRINT AREA

1. Set the print area and make active the worksheet it is on.

2. Click **Print** on the Standard toolbar.

TIP

If a worksheet has a print area, by default it will print instead of the full worksheet.

ADD CELLS TO A PRINT AREA:

1. Open **View** and click **Page Break Preview**.

2. Select the additional cells on the same worksheet you to want to print.

3. Right-click the selection and click **Add To Print Area**.

REMOVE ADDED CELLS FROM A PRINT AREA

1. Open **View** and click **Page Break Preview**.

2. Select the previously added cells you want to remove from the print area.

3. Right-click the selection, and click **Exclude From Print Area**.

REMOVE A PRINT AREA

1. Open **File**, point at **Print Area**, and click **Clear Print Area**.

   –Or–

   Open **View** and click **Page Break Preview**.

2. Right-click anywhere on the Page Break Preview worksheet, and click **Reset Print Area**.

   –Or–

   Open **File**, select **Page Setup**, and click the **Sheet** tab.

3. Select the text in the Print Area text box, and press DELETE.

4. Click **OK**.

Preview the Print Job

Before your printer actually starts printing paper, you can verify what you have set up to print. Print Preview displays replicas of the printed pages your data will produce, provides a hub for most printing features, and can be used as a printing starting point, as shown in Figure 5-5.

To open Print Preview:

- Click **Print Preview** on the Standard toolbar or in the Page Setup dialog box.

  –Or–

- Click **Preview** in the Print dialog box.

The buttons on the Print Preview toolbar provide tools to use in the window and links to other printing features.

- **Next** and **Previous** let you navigate between multiple pages.

- **Zoom** toggles between a full-page view and a magnified view of the current page. When viewing the full page, just click the Magnifier pointer anywhere to switch to the magnified view.

- **Print** opens the Print dialog box.

- **Setup** opens the Sheet tab of the Page Setup dialog box.

- **Margins** turns off or on visible margin lines that can be dragged to the position you want.

- **Page Break Preview** displays the active worksheet divided by pages. You can interactively change where page breaks occur, within the limits of your page size.

- **Normal View (alternates with Page Break Preview)** returns the view to a full worksheet with menus and toolbars when working in Page Break Preview.

- **Close** returns the view to a full worksheet with menus and toolbars.

- **Help** provides a review of the other button functions.

Figure 5-5: Print Preview shows replicas of printed pages and provides tools and features to verify and modify your print options prior to sending the job to the printer

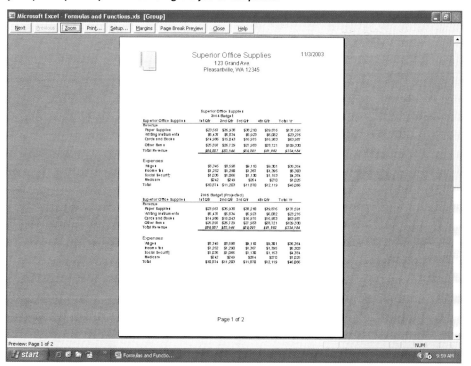

SET MARGINS INTERACTIVELY

1. Open **Print Preview**.

2. Click **Zoom**, if necessary, to show the first page of the worksheet in full-page view.

3. Click **Margins**, if necessary, to show six margin lines and handles, and column width handles, as shown in Figure 5-6.

4. Point at a line or handle until the cursor becomes a cross with either horizontal or vertical arrowheads, and drag the line or handle to set a new margin or column width. All pages use the same margin or column settings.

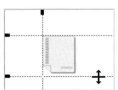

5. Either:

- Click **Close** to return to the normal worksheet view.

   –Or–

- Click **Page Break Preview** to adjust where data is separated into pages.

   –Or–

- Click **Setup** to open the Page Setup dialog box and choose from several printing options.

   –Or–

- Click **Print** to finalize print options before sending the print job to the printer.

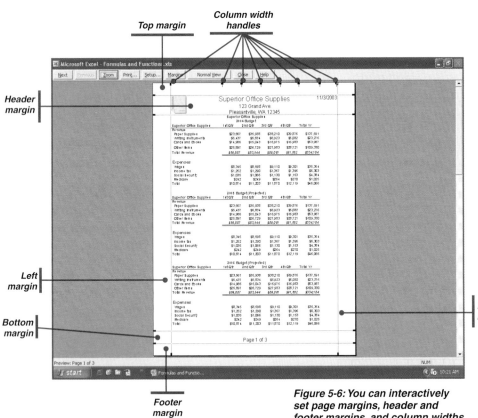

Figure 5-6: You can interactively set page margins, header and footer margins, and column widths

ADJUST PAGE BREAKS

You can adjust page breaks using Page Break Preview.

1. To open Page Break Preview:

- Open **Print Preview** and click **Page Break Preview**.

–Or–

- Open **View** and click **Page Break Preview**.

In either case, you see a welcome message.

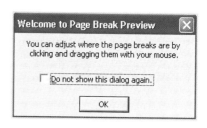

2. Click **Do Not Show This Dialog Again**, if that's what you want. In any case, click **OK**. The worksheet opens in a condensed format, as shown in Figure 5-7. Dashed lines show page breaks where Excel will separate data into pages; page break lines you move or add are shown as solid lines (outer boundary lines are also solid lines).

3. Do one or more:

- Adjust page breaks by dragging a line to where you want the page break. Dashed lines become solid after you move them from their default locations.

- Insert a page break by selecting the row below or the column to the right of where you want the new page break, right-clicking, and clicking **Insert Page Break**.

- Remove a page break by dragging it from the worksheet area to the dark gray area.

- Remove all page breaks you added or changed by right-clicking the worksheet and clicking **Reset All Page Breaks**.

4. To close Page Break Preview, either:

- Open **View** and click **Normal**.

–Or–

- Click **Print Preview** on the Standard toolbar, and then click **Normal View**.

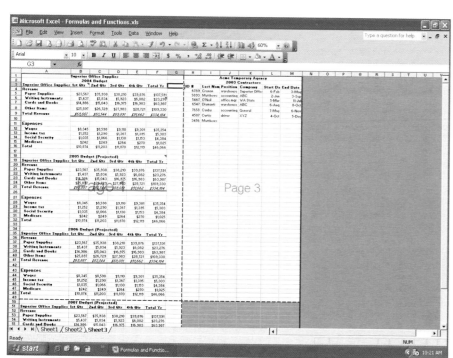

Figure 5-7: Dashed lines show page breaks in Page Break Preview

Output the Print Job

You can print to printers attached to your computer or printers on your network. You can also print to a file instead of a printer and choose features provided by your printer manufacturer. All this is accomplished from the Print dialog box, as shown in Figure 5-8, viewed by opening **File** and clicking **Print**, or by pressing **CTRL+P**.

CHOOSE A PRINTER

Either:

- In the Printer area, click the **Name** down arrow and select a printer that is installed on your computer from the drop-down list.

—Or—

- If you are part of a domain with Active Directory, click the Find Printer button to locate a shared printer on your network. After choosing a printer, click **OK** to return to the Print dialog box.

In either case, the printer name is displayed in the Name drop-down list box, and information about the printer is listed below it.

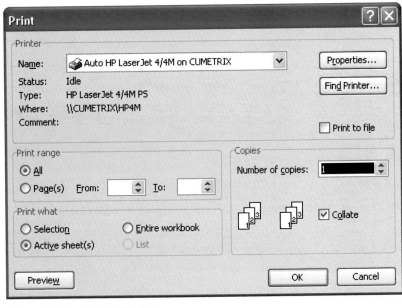

Figure 5-8: The Print dialog box provides options that control the physical aspects of printing

PRINT TO A FILE

You can print your printer information to a file instead of directly to a physical device. Print files are typically used to create Adobe PDF documents (you must select a PostScript printer in the Name box) or when you want to create a file of the print job to send to another computer.

1. Select **Print To File** and click **OK**.

2. In the Print To File dialog box, type the path and file name where you want the print file located, and click **OK**.

Figure 5-9: Printers may have additional printing features besides those provided in Excel

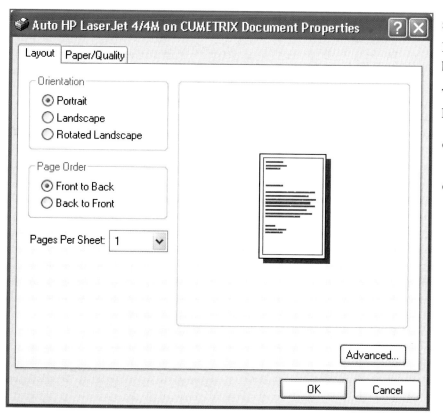

SELECT PRINTER-SPECIFIC OPTIONS

Most printers have additional printing options and features besides those provided in Excel.

To display a printer's properties dialog box, as shown in Figure 5-9, either:

● Click **Properties** in the Print dialog box.

–Or–

● Click **Options** in the Page Setup dialog box.

PRINT MULTIPLE COPIES

1. In the Copies area, adjust the **Number Of Copies** spinner to the number of copies you want.

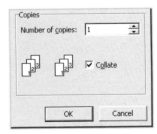

2. Then either:

   • Select **Collate,** to print each copy from start to finish before starting to print the next copy.

   –Or–

   • Deselect **Collate**, to print each page the number of times set in the Number Of Copies spinner before printing the next page.

Chapter 6

Charting Data

In this chapter you will learn how to display worksheet data graphically in what Excel calls charts. Providing a more visual representation of data than a worksheet grid, charts show trends and comparisons at a quick glance. Figure 6-1 shows a column chart, typically used to compare the values of two or more categories, and many of the elements (or items) that can be used on a chart.

Charts can be created manually or by using a wizard. Each chart can be refined as you are setting it up or after it appears on the worksheet. Display options are also available that allow you to hide data you may not want to display and permit you to choose whether to show the chart on the same worksheet as its underlying data or in a separate chart sheet. These, along with other things you can do with charts, are covered in the following sections.

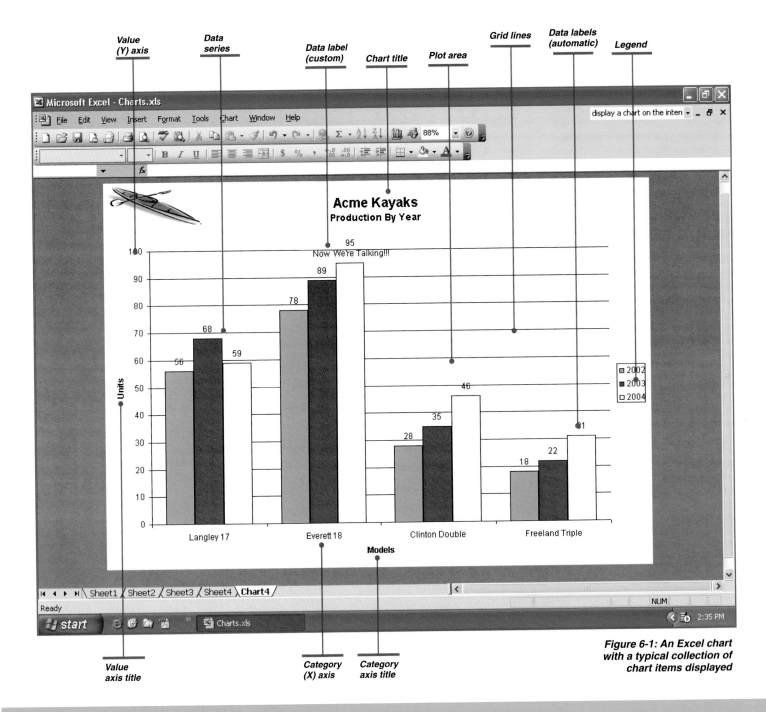

Figure 6-1: An Excel chart with a typical collection of chart items displayed

The first step in the Chart Wizard can also be its last. At any time in the process of working your way through the wizard, when you feel like you have what you want, just click **Finish**. There's really nothing to lose but a little time, as you can easily delete the chart that's been produced and start over again. The Chart Wizard, like wizards in general, allows you to go back to a previous step, make a change, and pick up where you left off.

Build a Chart with the Chart Wizard

Microsoft has worked hard to make the mechanics of creating charts relatively painless. This section shows you how to create a chart by using a wizard and provides chart-building information that can be applied as you further learn to build a chart manually.

Start the Chart Wizard

Click the **Chart Wizard** button on the Standard toolbar. The Chart Wizard dialog box opens to Chart Type, the first step in the process of creating a chart, as shown in Figure 6-2.

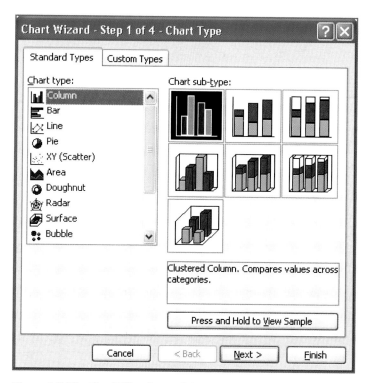

Figure 6-2: The Chart Wizard gets right to work by asking you to choose a chart type

Choose a Chart Type

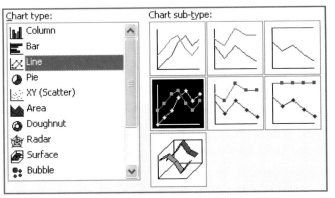

Figure 6-3: A Line chart has seven variations, or sub-types

Excel organizes it charts into 14 standard types and ten custom chart types. It also has a repository in which you can store the unique types of your own making. Within each standard chart type are more variations called sub-types. For example, the Line chart type has seven ways to display trends, as shown in Figure 6-3. Custom charts are standard charts that are used for a specific purpose, such as the Pie Explosion chart, which is basically the same as one of the Pie sub-types but is optimized for PowerPoint presentations. All totaled, you have 93 standard and custom chart types to choose from and a virtually unlimited number of user-defined charts you can set up. The main chart categories are summarized in Table 6-1.

CHART TYPE	FUNCTION
Standard Charts:	
Column, Bar, Line Cylinder, Cone, Pyramid	Compare trends in multiple data series in various configurations, such as vertical, horizontal; and in several shapes, such as bar, cylinder, cone, and pyramid
Pie and Doughnut	Display one data series (pie) or compare multiple data series (doughnut) as part of a whole, or 100 percent
XY (Scatter)	Displays pairs of data to establish concentrations
Area	Shows the magnitude of change over time; useful when summing multiple values to see the contribution of each
Radar	Connects changes in a data series from a starting or center point with lines, markers, or a colored fill
Surface	Compares trends in multiple data series in a continuous curve; similar to Line chart with a 3-D visual effect
Bubble	Displays sets of three values; similar to an XY chart with the third value being the size of the bubble
Stock	Displays three sets of values, such as a high, low, and closing stock price
Custom Charts	Variations on standard charts, Custom Charts are one of a kind for which there are no sub-types and which are typically used for a specific application. For example, the Logarithmic chart is a line chart with a special scale, while the Column-Area or Line-Column charts are combinations of two standard charts.
User-Defined Charts	Charts that include formatting and unique settings that you might want to save to apply to future charts.

TABLE 6-1: *The Dozens of Excel Charts Can Be Categorized by Function*

1. In the Chart Wizard Step 1 of 4 Chart Type dialog box, select the type of chart you want.

2. To help you choose a chart type, review Table 6-1 and/or select several chart types to read their descriptions as they are displayed in the dialog box.

3. Use the **Press And Hold To View Sample** button to get a glimpse of how the selected chart will look with your data.

> Press and Hold to View Sample

4. Click **Next** when you have made your choice.

Select Data for Charting

Charts are created from selected worksheet data. Excel makes assumptions on how to set up the plot area, assign axes, and make labels based on the data. Though you can change many of the chart items after the chart is created and Excel will quickly reconfigure the chart, it speeds things along (and increases the likelihood of seeing what you want!) if the data is properly organized. Guidelines for setting up data for charting and assumptions Excel uses include:

- The selected data must be a rectangular *data range* or consist of multiple selections.

- Text, which is used solely to create labels, should only be in the topmost row and/or the leftmost column; otherwise, text encountered within the range is charted as zero.

- Each cell must contain a *value* (or data point). Values in the same row or column are considered to be related and are called a *data series*. The first data series starts with the first cell in the upper-left of the selected data that is not text or formatted as a date. Subsequent data series are determined by Excel, continuing across the rows or down the columns.

- As Excel determines whether there are more rows or columns selected, it will assume the lesser number to be the data series and the greater number to be categories that are plotted on the category (X) axis. In Figure 6-4, three columns and four rows of data are selected; therefore, Excel plots the three years' of values each as a data series and considers the rows to be categories.

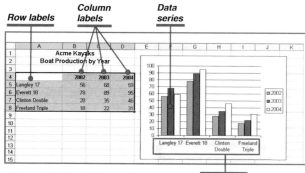

Figure 6-4: Excel determines whether row or column labels become the plotted data series by choosing the lesser number for the data series and the greater for categories

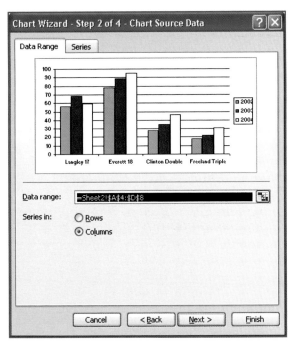

Figure 6-5: You can change whether the data series is plotted from row or columns and immediately see the difference

SELECT THE DATA RANGE

1. In the Chart Wizard Step 2 of 4 Source Data dialog box, click the **Data Range** tab.

2. Click the **Collapse Dialog** button at the right end of the Data Range text box to hide most of the dialog box.

3. Select the data range, including labels if they are in the topmost row or leftmost column.

	A	B	C	D
1	Acme Kayaks			
2	Boat Production by Year			
3				
4		2002	2003	2004
5	Langley 17	56	68	59
6	Everett 18	78	89	95
7	Clinton Double	28	35	46
8	Freeland Triple	18	22	31

4. Click the **Expand Dialog** button to return the wizard dialog box to its full size. Your selected range appears in the Data Range text box, and a sample of your charted data is displayed, as shown in Figure 6-5.

5. Click **Next**, if the chart displays as you want.

   –Or–

   Under Series In, change whether the series is produced from rows or columns. The change is immediately displayed in the sample area. Click **Next**, if the chart displays as you want.

6. If you need to add or remove data series, click the **Series** tab. See "Modify the Data Series" next.

TIP

Instead of clicking **Collapse Dialog**, dragging the area, and then clicking **Expand Dialog**, you can just start dragging the area, causing the dialog box to automatically collapse. It will expand again when you are done.

NOTE

The series name and values you choose can be from other worksheets or open workbooks. All you are really doing is adding more information to the chart that is not within your originally selected data.

MODIFY THE DATA SERIES

Without affecting any of the underlying data, you can add or remove data series, select the cells that identify the data series' name and the data series' value, and change which cells are used for labels for the category (X) axis.

1. In the Chart Wizard Step 2 of 4 Source Data dialog box, click the **Series** tab.

2. In the Series list box:

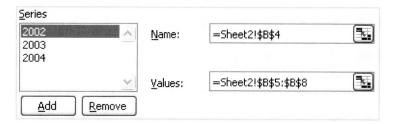

- Select a current series to change its name or values location.

 –Or–

 - Click **Add** or **Remove** to start a new series or remove an existing one.

3. In the Name text box, click the **Collapse Dialog** button, and select the cell that contains the text you want for the selected series. Click the **Expand Dialog** button to return to the full dialog box.

4. In the Values text box, click the **Collapse Dialog** button, and select the cells that contain the values you want plotted for the selected series. Click the **Expand Dialog** button to return to the full dialog box.

5. If needed, change the category axis labels by selecting the cells that contain the label names.

6. Click **Next** when the chart is looking how you want.

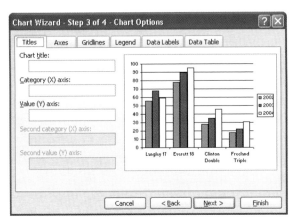

Figure 6-6: The Chart Options dialog box provides formatting and other options tailored to the type of chart you are working on

Modify Chart Items

The Chart Wizard's third step lets you customize many of the items that comprise the chart, as shown in Figure 6-6. Click one or more tabs whose item you want to change. Make any changes you want, and then click **Next**. See "Format Chart Items" later in the chapter.

Choose a Chart Location

You can display charts you create as an object on a worksheet (*embedded chart*), or you can devote a full worksheet, or chart sheet, to the chart.

1. In the Chart Wizard Step 4 of 4 - Chart Location dialog box, either:

   ● Click **As New Sheet** to create a new worksheet with the chart as its sole content, as shown in Figure 6-7. Select the default worksheet name and type your own.

   –Or–

   ● Click **As Object In** to create an embedded chart, shown in Figure 6-8. Select the worksheet from the active workbook where you want the chart placed. You can treat the embedded chart as you do other objects, such as pictures. For example, you can size, move, and copy and paste the chart.

2. Click **OK**. Along with chart, a floating chart toolbar is displayed, which is described in the next section.

TIP

The Category (X) axis is across the bottom of most charts, like the kayak models shown in the example chart in Figure 6-6. The Values (Y) axis is up the left side, like the units in the example.

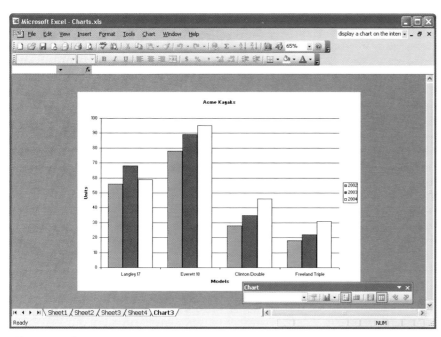

Figure 6-7: Chart sheets display charts
on their own worksheets

Figure 6-8: Embedded charts are
objects placed on a worksheet

NOTE

Each of the dialog boxes that make up the four steps in
the Chart Wizard are available as menu commands and
can be used to change chart items on existing charts that
were created by the wizard or charts created from the
Chart toolbar, described in the next section. The wizard's
predominate role is to assist you in the chart building
flow. Once you are comfortable with how to get started
building a chart, you might find the techniques described
in the next section more efficient.

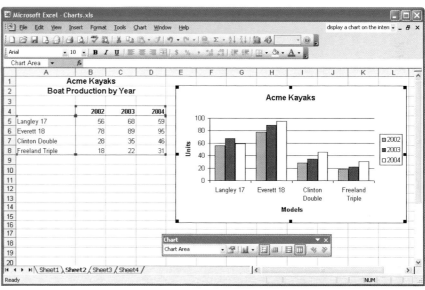

Modify Existing Charts

Excel treats each item of a chart uniquely; that is, each has its own set of formatting and other characteristics you can apply. Once you have a basic chart displayed, you can totally redesign it by selecting and changing each of its component pieces. This section starts with an alternative to using the Chart Wizard and then shows you how to customize the items that comprise a chart.

Create a Chart from the Chart Toolbar

The Chart toolbar provides access to many of the same tools and options as the Chart Wizard, though after the chart is displayed, you are on your own to change items without the benefit of the wizard guiding you along.

1. To display the Chart toolbar, open **View**, point at **Toolbars**, and click **Chart**. A floating Chart toolbar is displayed, as shown in Figure 6-9.

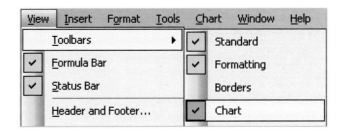

2. Select the data you want to chart.

3. Click the **Chart Type** down arrow, and click the chart type you want. The chart is displayed.

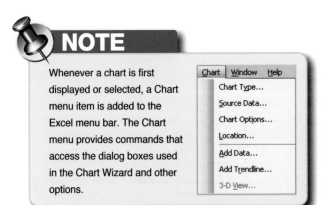

TIP

To *dock* the floating toolbar with the other toolbars at the top of the Excel window, double-click the toolbar's title bar.

NOTE

Whenever a chart is first displayed or selected, a Chart menu item is added to the Excel menu bar. The Chart menu provides commands that access the dialog boxes used in the Chart Wizard and other options.

QUICKSTEPS

SELECTING CHART ITEMS

You can select items using a toolbar, keyboard, or by clicking an item with the mouse. When selected, items will display small rectangular handles (for some items these are sizing handles; for others, they just show selection).

SELECT CHART ITEMS FROM THE CHART TOOLBAR

1. Click the chart you are working on.
2. Display the Chart toolbar by right-clicking a toolbar and clicking **Chart**.

3. Click the **Chart Objects** down arrow to open its drop-down list and click the item you want to select.

SELECT CHART ITEMS USING THE KEYBOARD

1. Click the chart.
2. Use the arrow keys to cycle through the chart items. The name of the selected item is shown in the Chart Objects drop-down list on the Chart toolbar.

SELECT CHART ITEMS BY CLICKING

Place the mouse pointer over the item you want selected, and click.

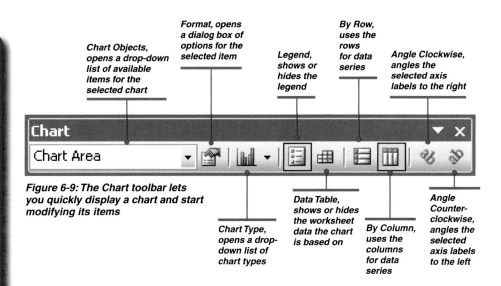

Chart Objects, opens a drop-down list of available items for the selected chart

Format, opens a dialog box of options for the selected item

Legend, shows or hides the legend

By Row, uses the rows for data series

Angle Clockwise, angles the selected axis labels to the right

Chart Type, opens a drop-down list of chart types

Data Table, shows or hides the worksheet data the chart is based on

By Column, uses the columns for data series

Angle Counter-clockwise, angles the selected axis labels to the left

Figure 6-9: The Chart toolbar lets you quickly display a chart and start modifying its items

Identify Items

It's easy to confuse which item is selected on a chart, especially on more complex charts with multiple series and axes. Excel provides several clues as to the identity of the selected item and, if applicable to the item, its value and data. Click an item to see its particulars:

- On the ScreenTip of the item

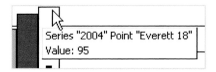

- In the Chart Objects text box on the Chart toolbar

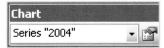

- In the Name box on the Formula bar

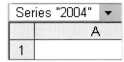

TIP

You can add a second category and/or value axis that can have its own title. A second axis is typically used when the values in one data series is proportionately a lot different from the others and needs a different scale of values. See "Add a Second Value Axis" later in the chapter.

- In the Formula bar

  fx =SERIES(Sheet2!D4

- Color coded on the worksheet

2002	2003	2004
56	68	59
78	89	95
28	35	46
18	22	31

Value axis title   *Chart title*

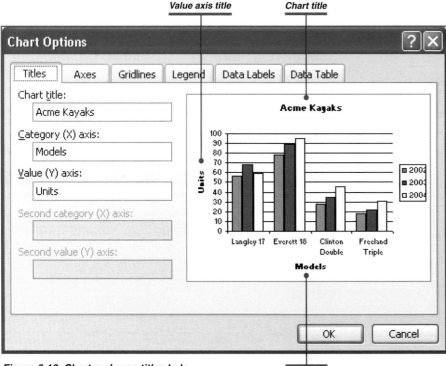

Figure 6-10: Chart and axes titles help clarify data displayed on a chart

Category axis title

Add Titles

Titles help readers quickly orient themselves to the data being presented.

1. Click the chart.

2. Open **Chart**, select **Chart Options**, and click the **Titles** tab.

3. Type titles for the chart and category and value axes. They are added to your chart sample, as shown in Figure 6-10.

4. Click **OK**.

Show or Hide Axes

The primary category (X) and value (Y) axes can be displayed or not depending on whether the information provided adds value to your chart.

1. Click the chart.
2. Open **Chart**, select **Chart Options**, and click the **Axes** tab.
3. To show the category axis, select its check box and choose one of the data-dependent options:

- **Automatic** tells Excel to display the scale as a time-scale if the underlying data is date formatted, or as categories otherwise.

- **Category** tells Excel to display the axis as categories.

- **Time-Scale** tells Excel to display the axis with a time-scale.

4. To show the value axis, select its check box.
5. Click **OK**.

Add or Remove Gridlines

Gridlines provide a background reference to value and category axes intervals. You can choose to have a few gridlines at what Excel determines are the major intervals, such as every 10 values on a value scale of 0-100; and/or at minor intervals, such as at every other value on a value scale of 0-100; or not at all.

1. Click the chart.
2. Open **Chart**, select **Chart Options**, and click the **Gridlines** tab.
3. Select the axis and interval of gridlines you want.

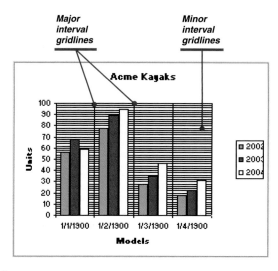

Major interval gridlines

Minor interval gridlines

4. Click **OK**.

Show or Hide a Legend

A *legend* identifies the data series in a chart. You can choose to display the legend or not, and where on the chart the legend is located.

1. Click the chart.

2. Open **Chart**, select **Chart Options**, and click the **Legend** tab.

3. Either:

- Deselect the check box next to Show Legend to hide the legend.

–Or–

- Select the check box next to Show Legend to show the legend, and click a placement location.

4. Click **OK**.

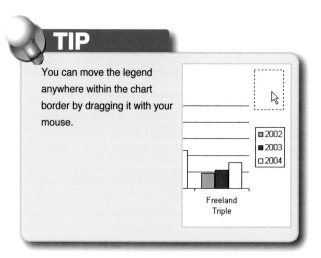

TIP

You can move the legend anywhere within the chart border by dragging it with your mouse.

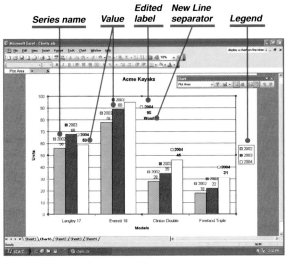

Series name | Value | Edited label | New Line separator | Legend

Figure 6-11: Data labels add another level of detail to a chart

Add Data Labels

Data series are identified in the legend, but if you want labels shown directly on the plot area in addition to or instead of having a legend, you can add them.

1. Click the chart.

2. Open **Chart**, select **Chart Options**, and click the **Data Labels** tab.

3. In the Label Contains area, select one or more criteria that will be displayed.

Label Contains
- ☑ Series name
- ☐ Category name
- ☐ Value

4. Optionally:

   ● Open the **Separator** drop-down list, and choose how you want to provide separation between multiple labels.

   ● Select **Legend Key** to provide a color-coded rectangle near each data series that corresponds to the legend label.

5. Click **OK**. (Figure 6-11 shows a chart with several data label possibilities.)

Display the Data Table

You can add the selected worksheet data, or *data table*, to the chart area.

1. Click the chart.

2. Open **Chart**, select **Chart Options**, and click the **Data Table** tab.

3. Select **Show Data Table**.

4. Optionally, select **Show Legend Keys** to add a column containing the legend labels and color codes.

5. Click **OK**. The data table is added to the chart area below the plot area.

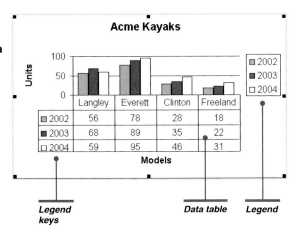

Acme Kayaks

	Langley	Everett	Clinton	Freeland
■ 2002	56	78	28	18
■ 2003	68	89	35	22
☐ 2004	59	95	46	31

Models

Legend keys | Data table | Legend

Format Chart Items

Each chart item has an associated Format dialog box with one or more tabs that provide formatting options. Several of the chart items have identical or a very similar set of formatting options. Table 6-2 shows the formatting options, organized by tabs that display in the individual Format dialog boxes, and the chart items that apply.

FORMATTING OPTIONS (BY TAB)	DESCRIPTION	APPLY TO:
Patterns	Adds borders and backgrounds, tick mark styles and labels, and table layout options	Titles, Legends, Chart Area, Axes, Gridlines, Data Series, Data Labels, Plot Area, Data Table
Font	Changes the font, font style, font size, color, and other effects of characters	Titles, Legends, Chart Area, Axes, Data Labels, Data Table
Alignment	Rotates text and controls text direction (for several Middle Eastern and East Asian languages)	Titles, Legends, Axes, Data Labels
Properties	Controls how the object moves, how it is sized, and whether it prints	Chart Area
Scale	Provides scaling parameters, such as start and end values, interval between minor and major units, and where the axes cross	Axes, Gridlines
Number	Provides the same number formats as the Format Cells Number tab, such as currency, accounting, date, and time	Axes, Data Labels
Placement	Provides location options on the chart	Legend
Axis	Plots the series on a secondary axis	Data Series
Y Error Bars	Graphically displays error notations (plus, minus, or both) from a plotted value and sets the error amount	Data Series
Data Labels	Allows you to set the label to series name, category name, value, and other criteria	Data Series
Series Order	Sets the order that the series are plotted (example: if you plotted three consecutive years, you could plot them in reverse order)	Data Series
Options	Provides the gap spacing between categories, overlap of data series columns or bars, and color variation	Data Series

TABLE 6-2: *Each Chart Item Has Its Own Collection of Formatting Options*

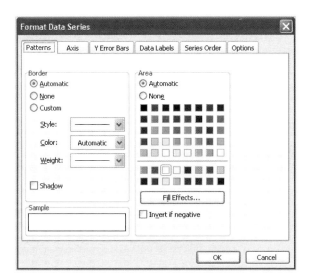

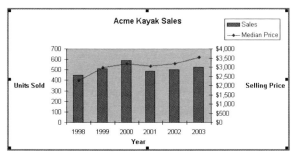

Figure 6-12: Two value axes allow you to combine two different data series on one chart to ascertain relationships

To format a chart item:

1. Right-click the item and click **Format *chart item***, or double-click the item. A Format dialog box tailored to that item opens.

2. Find the formatting option category you want from Table 6-2.

3. Click the tab that contains the formatting option you want to apply.

4. Select and/or adjust the formatting option, and click **OK**.

Add a Second Value Axis

When you have data series that contain values (or data points) with disproportional or different types of values, you might need to create a second value axis to keep the scaling meaningful.

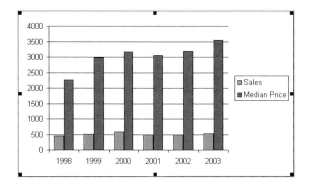

1. Click the chart.

2. Open **Chart**, select **Chart Type**, and click the **Custom Types** tab.

3. In the Chart Type list box, click **Line-Column On 2 Axes** (or another applicable chart type), and click **OK**. The chart reconfigures with a second value axis, and one series is shown as a column with the other as a line, as shown in Figure 6-12.

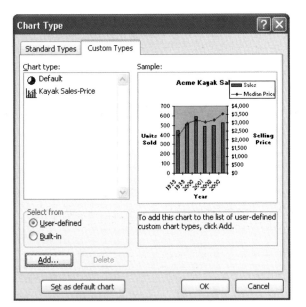

Figure 6-13: Your user-defined chart appears in the Chart Type dialog box just like the standard and custom charts Excel provides

Create Your Own Chart Type

After you have applied formatting and added or removed chart items, your chart may not resemble any of the standard or even custom chart types provided by Excel. To save your work so you can build a similar chart at another time:

1. Build the chart and then select it.

2. Open **Chart**, select **Chart Type**, and click the **Custom Types** tab.

3. In the Select From area, click **User-Defined**, then click **Add**. The Add Custom Chart Type dialog box opens.

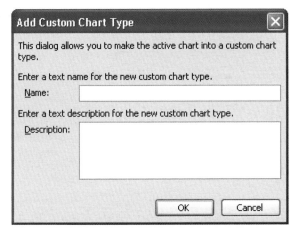

4. Type a name and description for the chart, and click **OK**. The chart appears as a user-defined chart type that you can choose in the future, as shown in Figure 6-13. Click **OK** to close the Chart Type dialog box.

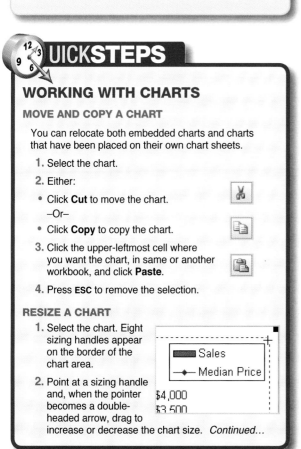

NOTE

When charts are copied or moved, they maintain a relationship with their underlying worksheet data. Charts and underlying data tables in the same workbook are updated according to your calculation settings in the Calculation tab of the Tools menu Options dialog box. When charts and their underlying data are in different workbooks, updates occur just as when they are in the same worksheet—if all workbooks are open. Charts in closed workbooks are updated when you next open them.

QUICKSTEPS

WORKING WITH CHARTS

MOVE AND COPY A CHART

You can relocate both embedded charts and charts that have been placed on their own chart sheets.

1. Select the chart.
2. Either:
   - Click **Cut** to move the chart.
   –Or–
   - Click **Copy** to copy the chart.
3. Click the upper-leftmost cell where you want the chart, in same or another workbook, and click **Paste**.
4. Press **ESC** to remove the selection.

RESIZE A CHART

1. Select the chart. Eight sizing handles appear on the border of the chart area.
2. Point at a sizing handle and, when the pointer becomes a double-headed arrow, drag to increase or decrease the chart size. *Continued...*

Use Charts

Charts can be moved, copied, printed, and enhanced with pictures, text, and trendlines. Some chart types even can be pulled apart and rotated.

Add Pictures and Text

Pictures and text can often bring focus to a chart.

ADD PICTURES

Photos, clip art, and other pictures can be added to a chart. The following steps show how to add clip art from the Office collection.

1. Click the chart.
2. Open **Insert**, point at **Picture**, and click **Clip Art**. The Clip Art task pane opens.
3. Type a keyword in Search For. You can narrow the search by choosing specific collections in which to search in Search In and by selecting only **Clip Art** in Results Should Be.
4. Click **Go**. After a few moments picture thumbnails start displaying.
5. Locate and double-click the picture you want. The picture appears in the upper-left corner of the chart area.
6. Size the picture by dragging one of its sizing handles. Move the picture by dragging the four-sided cross, as shown in Figure 6-14. (See Chapter 7 for more information on formatting pictures.)

WORKING WITH CHARTS: *(Continued)*

INSERT A CHART SHEET

1. Right-click the worksheet tab to the right of where you want the new chartsheet, and click **Insert**.

2. In the General tab, double-click the **Chart** icon.

3. Start the Chart Wizard and build the chart. The chart sheet is inserted and is named Chart *x*.

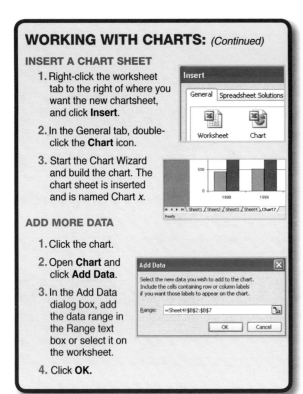

ADD MORE DATA

1. Click the chart.

2. Open **Chart** and click **Add Data**.

3. In the Add Data dialog box, add the data range in the Range text box or select it on the worksheet.

4. Click **OK**.

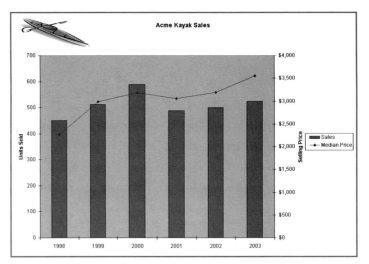

ADD TEXT

You can insert a text box and add text to a chart.

1. Click the chart.

2. Display the Drawing toolbar, if necessary. Click **Drawing** on the Standard toolbar to do that.

3. Click the **Text Box** button. Use the pointer to drag a box in the chart area to the approximate location and size you want.

4. Type your text. Use the sizing handles to resize the text box, and drag the border to move the text box.

5. Click outside the text box to see your results.

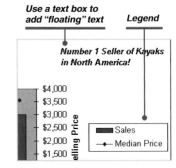

Add a Trendline

"Past performance does not guarantee future results," but Excel can analyze plotted data and predict a trend. To add a trendline to your chart:

1. Right-click a data series in the chart that you want analyzed, and click **Add Trendline**. The Add Trendline dialog box opens.

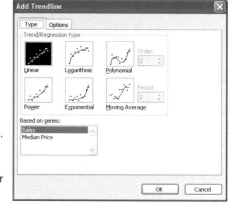

2. Accept the default Linear trend/regression (unless you are familiar with the other regressions), and in the Based On Series list box, click the series you want the trendline applied to.

3. Click the **Options** tab and either:

   ● Adjust the **Forward** Forecast spinner to the number of future time periods (incremented according to the time-scale axis on your chart) you want the trendline to forecast and display.

   –Or–

   ● Adjust the **Backward** Forecast spinner to the number of past time periods (incremented according to the time-scale axis on your chart) you want the trendline to display, showing what past results may have been.

4. Optionally, add a custom name to the trendline. Select or deselect the remaining options.

5. Click **OK**. A trendline is added to the chart, as shown in Figure 6-15, and its name appears in the legend, if shown.

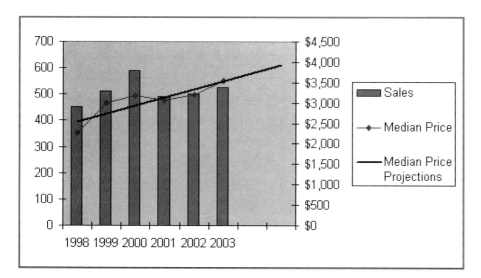

Figure 6-15: Trendlines can predict future results

Print a Chart

You can print a chart along with data and other worksheet objects, or you can choose to print just the chart.

PRINT A CHART WITH OTHER WORKSHEET INFORMATION

1. Size, move, copy, and otherwise position the embedded chart on the worksheet in conjunction with worksheet data and objects.

2. Click **Print Preview** on the Standard toolbar. Use the buttons along the Print Preview toolbar to set up print options, change margins, and adjust page breaks. (See Chapter 5 for more information on printing a worksheet.)

3. Click **Print**. In the Print dialog box, select a printer, determine which pages and how many to print.

4. Click **OK**.

PRINT A CHART ONLY

1. Select the embedded chart or a chart located on a chart sheet.

2. Open **File**, select **Page Setup**, and click the **Chart** tab, shown in Figure 6-16.

3. In the Printed Chart Size area, choose how large you want the chart.

4. In the Printing Quality area, choose options that might increase printing speed and/or decrease ink or toner.

5. Use any printing options described in Chapter 5. Click **Print Preview** and make final adjustments.

6. Click **Print**. In the Print dialog box, select a printer, determine which pages and how many to print.

7. Click **OK**.

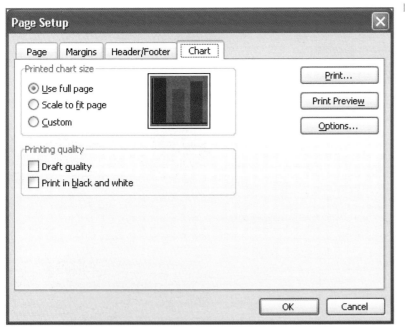

Figure 6-16: When printing only charts, you have sizing and quality options in addition to general printing options

NOTE

The steps described for rotating and separating pie slices also work for doughnut charts.

Work with Pie Charts

Pie charts have a few unique features that you can use to change how their component slices are viewed.

ROTATE SLICES

The slices of a pie chart are initially plotted according to the order of the worksheet data. You can rotate the orientation of the slice to emphasize (or de-emphasize!) certain data.

1. Right-click a data series in the pie chart, and click **Format Data Series**; or double-click a data series.

2. Click the **Options** tab. Increase the **Angle Of First Slice** spinner until the slices in the sample rotate to the positions you want.

3. Click **OK**.

SEPARATE SLICES

You can separate slices all at once or individually.

To separate all the slices in unison:

1. Click the pie. Each slice will display a selection handle.

2. Drag the center of the pie outward to create the separation distance you want.

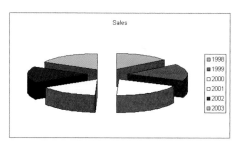

To separate individual slices:

1. Click the pie. Each slice will display a selection handle.

2. Click the slice you want to separate. Selection handles will surround the slice.

3. Drag the slice outward to create the separation distance you want.

4. Repeat Steps 4 and 5 for other slices.

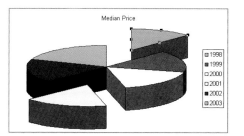

How to...

Chapter 7
Working with Graphics

Graphics is a term used to describe several forms of visual enhancements that can be added to a worksheet. In this chapter, you will learn how to insert, format, and manage graphic files (*pictures*), such as digital photos and clip art images. You will see how to create your own basic renderings (*drawings*) directly on a worksheet and how to combine them with built-in drawings (*shapes*). Additionally, you will see how to embed products of other programs (*objects*) alongside your data and how to produce organizational charts and other business-oriented *diagrams*.

Add Graphics

Excel uses a myriad of menus, dialog boxes, task panes, and toolbars to move graphics on to the worksheet, yet the central point of inserting graphics within Excel is the Drawing toolbar, shown in Figure 7-1.

After a graphic is placed on a worksheet, you have almost unlimited freedom to move and modify the graphic. See "Format and Modify Graphics" later in the chapter for ways to change inserted graphics.

Figure 7-1: The Drawing toolbar provides one-click access to adding graphics

Line, Arrow, Rectangle, Oval, and Text Box, provide tools to create your own graphics and add text

Insert WordArt, adds special effects to text

Insert Picture From File, allows you to browse for graphic files

Insert Clip Art, opens the gateway to search for clips and organize clip art collections

AutoShapes, opens several categories of shapes and connecting items

Insert Diagram or Organizational Chart, provides access to organizational chart tools and five business-related diagrams

TABLE 7-1: *Graphic Files Supported by Excel*

FILE TYPE	EXTENSION
Windows Bitmap	BMP, BMZ, RLE, DIB
Computer Graphics Metafile	CGM
CorelDRAW	CDR, CDT, CMX, PAT
Micrografx Designer/Draw	DRW
AutoCAD 2-D	DXF
Enhanced Metafile	EMF
Encapsulated PostScript	EPS
FPX	FPX
Graphics Interchange Format	GIF, GFA
Joint Photographic Expert Graphics	JPG, JPEG, JFIF, JPE
Picture It!	MIX
Macintosh PICT	PCT, PICT, PCZ
Portable Network Graphics	PNG
Tagged Image File Format	TIF, TIFF
Windows Metafile	WMF, WMZ
WordPerfect	WPG

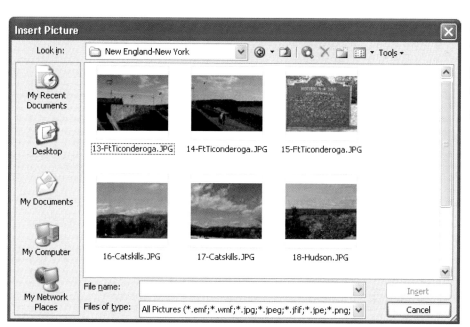

Figure 7-2: The Insert Picture dialog box displays thumbnails of graphic files accepted by Excel

Add Pictures

You can browse for picture files, use the Clip Art task pane to assist you, or import them directly from a scanner or digital camera.

BROWSE FOR PICTURES

1. Select the cell where you want the upper-leftmost corner of the picture.

2. Open **Insert**, point at **Picture**, and click **From File**.

    –Or–

    Click **Insert Picture From File** on the Drawing toolbar.

    The Insert Picture dialog box opens as shown in Figure 7-2.

3. Browse to the picture you want and select it. (If you do not see thumbnails of your pictures, click the **Views** down arrow on the dialog box toolbar, and click **Thumbnails**.)

4. Click **Insert**. The picture displays on the worksheet. (See "Resize and Rotate a Graphic," later in the chapter, to see how to resize the picture.)

ADD CLIP ART

1. Select the cell where you want the upper-leftmost corner of the picture.

2. Open **Insert**, point at **Picture**, and click **Clip Art**.

    –Or–

    Click **Insert Clip Art** on the Drawing toolbar.

    The Clip Art task pane opens.

3. In the **Search For** text box, type a keyword.

4. Click the **Search In** down arrow and refine your search to specific collections. (The Web Collections category includes thousands of clips maintained at Office Online; therefore, it can take considerable time to find what you're looking for.)

TIP

It's not terribly important to select a precise location for your inserted picture. You can easily move the picture into position by dragging it after it's displayed on your worksheet. See the QuickSteps, "Positioning Graphics," for information on moving and positioning graphics.

Figure 7-3: The Clip Art task pane helps you find clips on your computer and on Office Online and then assists you in organizing them

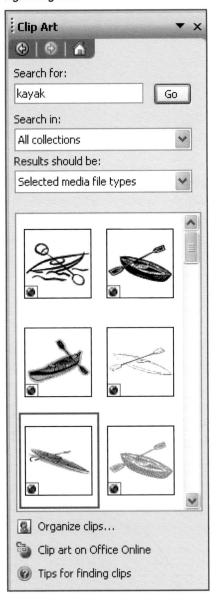

5. Click the **Results Should Be** down arrow and deselect all file types besides Clip Art.

6. Click **Go**. In a few moments thumbnails of the search results will appear, as shown in Figure 7-3.

7. Double-click the thumbnail to insert it on your worksheet. See the QuickSteps, "Using Clip Art."

ADD PICTURES DIRECTLY

1. Select the cell where you want the upper-leftmost corner of the picture.

2. Make sure the device, scanner or digital camera, is connected to your computer and is turned on.

3. Open **Insert**, point at **Picture**, and click **From Scanner Or Camera**. The Insert Picture From Scanner Or Camera dialog box opens.

4. Select the device you want to use.

5. Choose either:

   • **Web Quality** for a lower resolution (and smaller file size)

   –Or–

   • **Print Quality** for a high resolution image (and larger file size)

6. Select **Add Pictures To Click Organizer** if you think you might use the image again.

7. Insert the image by clicking:

   • **Insert** to add the image from the device with its default setting

   –Or–

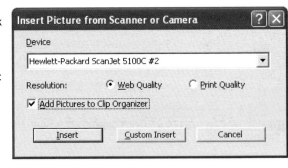

   • **Custom Insert** to choose from custom settings such as setting the resolution in dpi (dots per inch), adjusting brightness and contrast settings, and choosing to display the image in color, grayscale, or black and white. Figure 7-4 shows the advanced properties for a scanner.

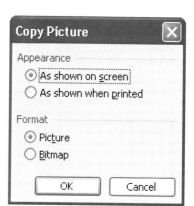

Figure 7-4: Depending on your device, you can set several image properties before you insert the image on to your worksheet

CREATE A PICTURE

You can create a picture from selected cells, a chart, or any other object on your worksheet and use them elsewhere.

1. Select what you want to become a picture.

2. Press and hold SHIFT, open **Edit**, and click **Copy Picture**. The Copy Picture dialog box opens. (Depending on the graphic selected, you may see additional options for Size.)

3. For closest representation of the selected items, choose the appearance/size to be **As Shown On Screen** and the format to be **Picture**.

4. Click **OK**.

5. Open the worksheet or other program, click where you want the picture, and click **Paste** on the Standard toolbar. Figure 7-5 shows a range as a picture in a PowerPoint slide.

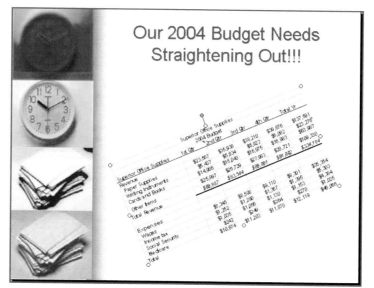

Figure 7-5: You can create a picture from worksheet data and objects and use it for other applications

Organize Clip Art

You can organize the clip art located on your hard disks into collections, entirely or by folders you choose. Keywords are automatically added to the clips so you can find them more easily.

1. If necessary, display the task pane by opening **View**, selecting **Toolbars**, and clicking **Task Pane**, or by simply pressing **CTRL+F1**.

2. Click the task pane title bar down arrow and select **Clip Art**. The Clip Art task pane opens, shown in Figure 7-3.

3. Click **Organize Clips**. The Add Clips To Organizer dialog box opens telling you the Microsoft Clip Organizer can search your hard disks and catalog any media files it finds. You can choose to do it now or later, and you can optionally pick the folders on your disks to be cataloged.

Figure 7-6: The Clip Organizer searches your hard disk and creates collections of clips similar to your folder structure

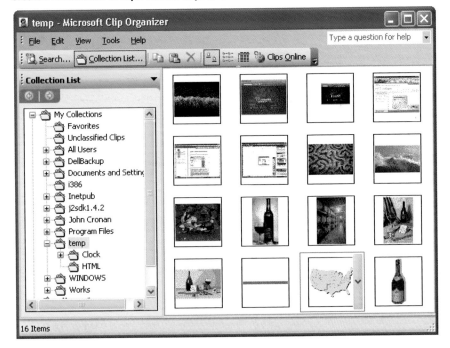

4. Click **Now**. After several moments of cataloging and adding keywords, the Microsoft Clip Organizer opens with your clips added to My Collections, similar to Figure 7-6. See the QuickSteps, "Using Clip Art," for information on managing and using clip art.

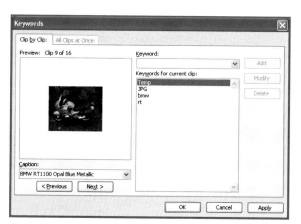

Figure 7-7: Add keywords for easier searching and captions to better describe your clip art

Use Clip Art

The Microsoft Clip Organizer is a Windows Explorer-type window that lets you perform many typical file and folder activities on your own clip art and clips provided by Microsoft Office. You can also acquire and transfer clips from online collections into your own.

OPEN THE CLIP ORGANIZER

Open the **Clip Art** task pane and click **Organize Clips**. The first time you do this you might want to catalog your clips. See "Organize Clip Art."

FIND CLIP ART

1. Click **Search**. A portion of the Clip Art task pane displays in the left pane of the window.

2. Add keywords in the **Search For** text box and refine the search in the **Search Options** drop-down list boxes.

3. Click **Go**. Clips meeting your search criteria display in the right pane.

MOVE AND COPY CLIPS IN A DIALOG BOX

1. Select a clip in the right pane, or to move and copy multiple clips, press and hold **CTRL** and click non-contiguous clips to select them, or press and hold **SHIFT** and click the first and last clip in a contiguous series. Click the down arrow of the clip, or one of the selected clips, or open the **Edit** menu.

2. Click **Copy To Collection** or **Move To Collection** depending on what you want to do.

3. In the Copy or Move dialog box, either browse to and select the collection where you want the clip and click **OK**, or put the clip into a new collection by clicking **New**, naming the collection, browsing to and selecting where you want the new collection, and clicking **OK** twice.

TIP

You can add clip art manually, from a camera or scanner, or automatically at any time. In the Clip Organizer, open **File**, select **Add Clips To Organizer**, and click the method of adding clips you want to use.

TIP

Actions you perform on clips in the Clip Organizer only affect what you see in the Organizer; that is, the actual graphic files located on your hard disks are not affected, and what you see in the Organizer are simply shortcuts to the files and folders themselves.

MOVE AND COPY CLIPS BY DRAGGING

1. Select a clip in the right pane, or to move and copy multiple clips, press and hold **CTRL** and click non-contiguous clips to select them, or press and hold **SHIFT** and click the first and last clip in a contiguous run.

2. Either copy the selected clips by dragging them from the right pane to the destination collection in the left pane, or move the selected clips by pressing and holding **SHIFT** while dragging them from the right pane to the destination collection in the left pane. Release the mouse before you release **SHIFT**.

DELETE CLIPS

1. Select a clip in the right pane, or to delete multiple clips, press and hold **CTRL** while clicking non-contiguous clips to select them, or press and hold **SHIFT** and click the first and last clip in a contiguous run. Click the down arrow of the clip or one of the selected clips, or open the **Edit** menu.

2. Click **Delete From** collection name to remove the clips from the current collection (if a clip was originally in My Collections, it is moved to the Unclassified Clips collection for future use; if the clip was added after your My Collection was created, it's removed from all collections), or click **Delete From Clip Organizer** to remove the clips from all collections.

EDIT KEYWORDS AND CAPTIONS

1. Select a clip in the right pane. Click its down arrow and click **Edit Keywords**. For adding keywords to multiple clips, select them, open **Edit**, and click **Keywords**.

2. In the Keywords dialog box, shown in Figure 7-7, click the **Clip By Clip** tab to address clips individually, or click the **All Clips At Once** tab to make changes to all selected clips.

3. Type keywords, separated by commas. Click **Add**. To delete a keyword, select it and click **Delete**.

4. Type a caption or select one from the drop-down list box. To delete a caption, select it and press **DELETE**.

1

2

3

4

5

6

7

8

9

10

Add AutoShapes

AutoShapes are small pre-built drawings you can select, or you can create your own by modifying existing shapes or drawing your own freeform. The pre-built AutoShapes and tools for creating your own are located together on the Drawing toolbar.

1. Click **Drawing** on the Standard toolbar to display the Drawing toolbar.

2. Choose an AutoShape:

   • Click **AutoShapes** and select a shape from one of the several categories.

   –Or–

   • Click one the four buttons to the right of AutoShapes to create lines, rectangles, and ellipses.

3. Drag your cross pointer in the approximate location and size you want. In the case of freeform tools, see the QuickSteps, "Working with Curves."

Add Objects from Other Programs

Much like including an Excel chart in a PowerPoint presentation or Access database, you might want to include the by-product of another program in a worksheet as a graphic. The big difference between adding the graphic as an *object* (these are technically *OLE objects*, named for "object linking and embedding," which is the technology involved) as opposed to copying and pasting it is that an object maintains a link to the program that created it. This means that in addition to formatting and other general appearance changes you can make with all the other graphics formats (see "Format and Modify Graphics" later in the chapter), you can make *content* changes using the menus, task panes, and other tools of the originating program while still in Excel.

QUICKSTEPS

WORKING WITH CURVES

Freeform tools are available to draw curved AutoShapes.

CREATE A CURVE

On the Drawing toolbar, click **AutoShapes**, and point at **Lines**. You may choose to:

- Click **Curve**, and click the cross pointer to establish the curve's starting point. Move the pointer and click to continue creating other curvatures. Double-click to set the end point and complete the drawing.

- Click **Scribble**, and drag the pencil icon to create the shape you want. Release the mouse button to complete the drawing.

- Click **Freeform**, and use a combination of curve and scribble techniques. Click the cross pointer to establish curvature points, and/or drag the pencil pointer to create other designs. Double-click to set the end point and complete the drawing.

ADJUST A CURVE

1. Right-click the curve and click **Edit Points**. Black rectangles (*vertices*) appear at the top of the curvature points.

2. Drag a vertex to reconfigure its shape.

3. Change any other vertex and click outside the curve when finished.

CLOSE A CURVE

Right-click the curve and click **Close Path**.

OPEN A CURVE

Right-click a closed curve and click **Open Path**.

1. Open **Insert** and click **Object**.

2. Choose whether to create a new object or use an existing one, as shown in Figure 7-8. Either:

   - Click the **Create New** tab, select an object type, and click **OK**.

     –Or–

   - Click the **Create From File** tab, browse to an existing object, and click **OK**.

Depending on the object, a blank object opens either in its originating program or within Excel, with the toolbars, menus, and other tools taking on those of the object's originating program.

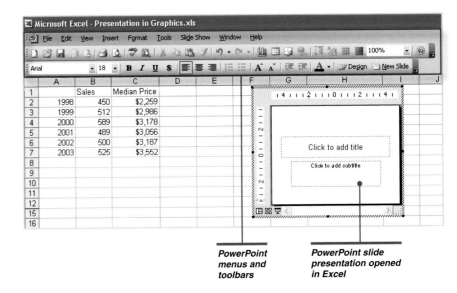

PowerPoint menus and toolbars

PowerPoint slide presentation opened in Excel

3. Add content, apply design and formatting. If you need to return to Excel, open the **File** menu, and click **Close And Return To** *object type* **In** *workbook name*; if you are already in Excel, just click the worksheet outside the object.

4. To edit the object or have it perform other actions, right-click the object, point at *type* **Object**, and click what you want it to do.

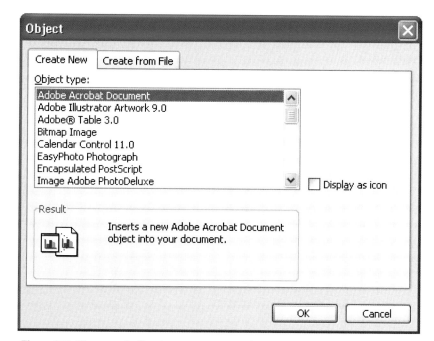

Figure 7-8: Choose whether to create a new object or browse to an existing one

Figure 7-9: The WordArt Gallery provides 30 special effects that can be applied to text

Add Special Effects to Text

Special effects, see Figure 7-9, can be easily added to text using WordArt to simulate a graphic artist's professional touch.

APPLY A WORDART EFFECT

1. Click the **Drawing** button on the Standard toolbar to display the Drawing toolbar.

2. Click the **WordArt** button to display the WordArt gallery of text styles.

3. Select a style that's close to what you want (you can "tweak" it later), and click **OK**. The Edit WordArt Text dialog box opens.

4. Type the text you want styled and click **OK**. The text is displayed with the effect you have selected.

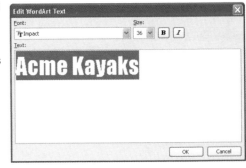

WORK WITH WORDART

A WordArt toolbar displays when you select text that has a WordArt effect applied to it. Use its buttons to edit, apply different styles, and change the contour of the effect. Do one or more of the following by clicking:

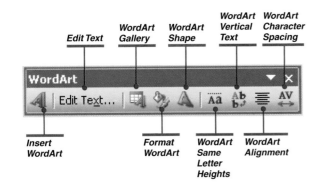

- **Insert WordArt**, to apply a WordArt effect to text (see "Apply a WordArt Effect")

- **Edit Text**, to change the text and its font characteristics that the effect is applied to

- **WordArt Gallery**, to apply a different effect to your text (see Figure 7-9)

- **Format WordArt**, to change formatting properties similar to the other graphic formats supported by Excel (see "Format Graphics" later in the chapter)

- **WordArt Shape**, to re-contour the WordArt effect to one of 40 different shapes

- **WordArt Same Letter Heights**, to adjust all WordArt characters to the same vertical size

- **WordArt Vertical Text**, to shift the positioning of WordArt characters to a vertical orientation from the typical horizontal orientation

- **WordArt Alignment**, to choose from several alignment formats

- **WordArt Character Spacing**, to choose from several spacing options

Create a Diagram

You can quickly create and modify several business-related diagrams, five of which are easily interchangeable. The sixth, an organization chart, provides special tools and features that streamline the structuring of this popular chart.

Click **Drawing** on the Standard toolbar and click **Insert Diagram Or Organizational Chart**, or open **Insert** and click **Diagram**. A gallery of diagrams opens.

ADD AN ORGANIZATIONAL CHART

Organization charts are particularly useful for showing hierarchical relationships, such as those found within a company. Double-click the upper-leftmost diagram to display the start of a chart and the Organization Chart toolbar. Then personalize your chart by doing one or more of the following:

- Click the highest level, or *manager* position, and click **Layout** to open a menu of hierarchical options. Click the structure that best matches your organization.

- Click the **Insert Shape** down arrow and pick where you want to add new positions to the current structure. To place text in a shape, place the insertion point in its text box. Type the name, title, or other identifier for the position. Press **ENTER** after each line of text to add multiple lines.

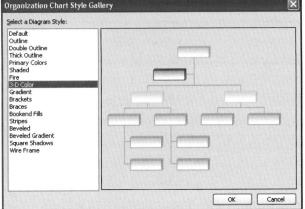

Figure 7-10: Quickly redesign the overall appearance of your organization chart

- Click **Select** to assist in selecting groups of positions that can be acted upon together.

- Click **AutoFormat** to open the Organization Chart Style Gallery, where you can change the overall appearance of the chart, as shown in Figure 7-10.

- Click the **Zoom** down arrow, and click a magnification factor to view the organization chart at a more macro and micro scale.

Co-workers are added on the same level as the selected position

Assistants are oriented below and off to one side of the selected position

Subordinates are placed under the selected position

INSERT A BASIC DIAGRAM

Double-click one of the five relationship or process diagrams in the Diagram Gallery dialog box. The diagram and a toolbar tailored to it are displayed. You may then personalize the diagram by doing one or more of the following:

- Click **Insert Shape** to add another copy of the selected shape to the diagram. To add text, place the insertion point in its text box. Type the name, title, or other identifier for the position. Press **ENTER** to add multiple lines.

- Click **Move Shape Backward/Forward** to move a selected shape from its relative position in the diagram.

- Click **Reverse Diagram** to change the direction of a flow (not particularly meaningful in non-process diagrams).

- Click **Layout** to resize the overall diagram

- Click **AutoFormat** to open the Diagram Style Gallery where you can change the overall appearance of the diagram.

- Click **Change To** to apply one of the four other basic diagram shapes to the current diagram. Click **Yes** if you see a message box that informs you AutoFormat needs to be turned on to continue.

NOTE

Diagrams are really just combinations of AutoShapes that fit a specific need. As such, you can, for example, delete an element of a diagram by selecting it and pressing **DELETE**, or delete the entire diagram by selecting its border and pressing **DELETE**. See the next section, "Format and Modify Graphics," to learn how to format the overall diagram as well as how to change various AutoShapes components.

Format and Modify Graphics

Excel makes formatting graphics a very intuitive and easy process, customizing the options you have available to the selected graphic. When a graphic is selected, a toolbar is displayed, tailored to the particular actions that are allowed to be performed on that particular graphic, see Figure 7-11 (except when shapes are selected, the Drawing toolbar isn't displayed, though the Drawing button on the Standard toolbar provides easy access).

In addition, whenever you double-click a graphic, a formatting properties dialog box is displayed, again tuned to the pertinent options of that graphic. Finally, the Drawing toolbar acts as a hub for accessing most of the graphic types, providing several alignment, distribution, and positioning tools for dealing with multiple graphics and displaying tools for coloring and styling.

Color, changes the graphic to grayscale, black and white, or to a washed-out look

Compress Pictures, lets you adjust the picture's resolution and file size

Set Transparency Color, allows you change the "see throughness" of backgrounds

Rotate Left 90°, turns the graphic counterclockwise

Insert Picture From File, provides a browse dialog box for adding pictures

More/Less Contrast, increases or reduces the contrast between dark and light

More/Less Brightness, increases or reduces brightness

Crop, allows you to trim the graphic

Line Style, allows you change the weight, style, and color of lines and borders

Format Picture, opens the picture's Format dialog box

Reset Picture, returns the graphic to its original settings

Picture

Figure 7-11: The Picture toolbar provides several formatting options for pictures, as do other toolbars that are displayed when you select their corresponding graphics

Use Color Effects

Color can be added to interior fills, to borders, and to text in various shades, gradients, textures, and patterns. Select the graphic and click the **Fill Color**, **Line Color**, or **Font Color** down arrow on the **Drawing** toolbar. A menu of coloring options displays. Depending on what attribute you want to format, you will see all or part of the following options.

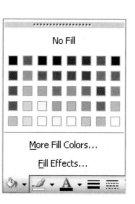

UICKSTEPS

USING HANDLES AND BORDERS TO CHANGE GRAPHICS

SELECT A GRAPHIC

How you select a graphic depends on whether the graphic is an image, a text box, or text in a text box.

- **Image**: Click the image. Handles appear around the graphic that allow you to perform interactive changes.

- **Text box**: Click the border of a text box. A dotted border appears around the perimeter of the text box.

  The fiscal 2005 projections seem somewhat optimistic...

- **Text in a text box**: Double-click an existing text box text to select it for making formatting changes, or click once in the text box where you want to place the insertion point for adding or editing text. In either case, the border becomes hatched.

  The fiscal 2005 projections seem somewhat optimistic...

RESIZE A GRAPHIC

Drag one of the round sizing handles surrounding the graphic—or at either end of it, in the case of a line—in the direction you want to enlarge or reduce the size of the graphic. Press and hold **SHIFT** when dragging a corner sizing handle to change the height and length proportionately. *Continued...*

SET A COLOR QUICKLY

Click one of the 40 primary colors in the color matrix on the drop-down menu to fill the graphic with the displayed color.

–Or–

Select **More Fill Colors** or **More Line Colors**, and click the **Standard** tab to have over 200 colors to choose from and adjust their transparency. Any current attribute color is shown along with your newly selected color. Click **OK** after making your choices.

SET A CUSTOM COLOR

1. Click **More Fill Colors** or **More Line Colors**, and click the **Custom** tab to adjust colors according to color models, as shown in Figure 7-12.

2. Click the color selection box to choose a color close to what you want.

3. Adjust the degree of light of the selected color with the slider to the right of the rainbow. The color will appear in the New area.

4. Choose the correct color model for your use (RGB is preferred for most general use and web graphics) and make any adjustments to the individual component color spinners.

5. Adjust the transparency and click **OK** when finished.

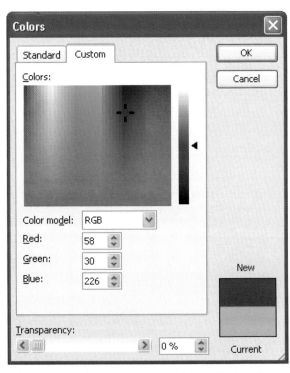

Figure 7-12: Adjust custom colors interactively or by setting the color values in the chosen color model

USING HANDLES AND BORDERS TO CHANGE GRAPHICS *(Continued)*

ROTATE A GRAPHIC

Drag the green dot in the direction you want to rotate. Press and hold **SHIFT** when dragging to rotate in 15° increments.

CHANGE A GRAPHIC'S PERSPECTIVE

If the graphic supports interactive adjustment, a yellow diamond adjustment handle is displayed. Drag the **yellow diamond** in or out to get the look you want.

SET GRADIENTS

1. Select **Fill Effects** and click the **Gradient** tab.
2. Select a Colors option:

   ● **One Color** gives you a one-color gradient result.

   ● **Two Colors** gives you a gradient resulting from one color blending into another.

   ● **Preset** allows you to select one of the gradient color schemes from the Preset Colors drop-down list box.

3. Select a Transparency percentage to set the degree of transparency:

   ● Click the horizontal arrows on **From** and **To**, to change the relative extent to which each extreme will be transparent.

   ● Click the **spinners** to set the degree of transparency more precisely.

4. Select a shading style to determine which direction the shading will fall across the graphic. To see the differences, click each option and see the results.

5. When you are done, click **OK**.

CREATE A TEXTURED BACKGROUND

1. Select **Fill Effects** and click the **Texture** tab.
2. Click the texture that you want to fill your graphic.
3. Click **OK**.

CREATE A PATTERNED BACKGROUND

1. Select **Fill Effects** and click the **Pattern** tab, or if working with lines, click **Patterned Lines**.
2. Select a pattern and then select your foreground and background colors. The resulting pattern will be reflected in the sample area.
3. When you are finished, click **OK**.

USE A PICTURE TO FILL YOUR GRAPHIC

1. Select **Fill Effects** and click the **Picture** tab.

2. Click **Select Picture**. The Select Picture dialog box will open.

3. Browse for the picture you want, select it, click **Insert**, and then click **OK**. The picture will be inserted into the background of the graphic shape.

COLOR TEXT BOX TEXT

1. Select the text to be colored by double-clicking or dragging. If you have trouble selecting the text you want, set your insertion point at the beginning or end of the selection, press and hold **CTRL+SHIFT** while using the arrow keys to select the remaining characters.

2. Click the **Font Color** down arrow and click the color you want from the color matrix. Your selected text is colored, and the toolbar button displays the selected color so you can apply that same color to additional objects by just clicking the button.

REMOVE EFFECTS

- To **remove a fill**, select the graphic, choose the **Fill Color** down arrow on the Drawing toolbar, and click **No Fill**.

- To **remove the outline border** around a graphic, select the graphic, choose the **Line Color down arrow** on the Drawing toolbar, and click **No Line**.

- To **remove text coloring**, select the text, choose the **Font Color** down arrow, and click **Automatic** to display black.

Resize and Rotate a Graphic

You can resize and rotate graphics quickly by dragging handles (see the QuickSteps, "Using Handles and Borders to Change Graphics"), or you can precisely set values in the Format dialog box, as shown in Figure 7-13. To do the latter:

1. Right-click the graphic, select **Format** *graphic*, and click the **Size** tab.

2. Resize the graphic by changing the **Height** and **Width** spinners in the:

  • **Size And Rotate** area, to change the size in units for each dimension

    –Or–

  • **Scale** area, to change the size in percentage for each dimension.

3. Adjust the **Rotation** spinner to rotate the graphic precisely. Positive degrees rotate clockwise; negative degrees rotate counterclockwise.

4. Select **Lock Aspect Ratio** to cause changes to affect the graphic proportionately to its height and width.

5. Select **Relative To Original Picture Size** to base changes on the original picture's dimensions; otherwise, they are based on the most recent change.

6. Click **Reset** if you need to get back to the previous or original size, and click **OK** when finished.

Trim a Picture

Pictures can be trimmed (*cropped*) by removing space from each of its sides. You can crop interactively or precisely.

  • To crop using the mouse, select the picture, and click the **Crop** button on the Picture toolbar. Point at a side or border and drag toward the center of the picture the amount you want to re-
move. Release the mouse button to com- 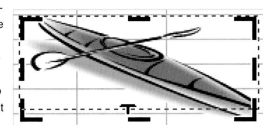 plete the crop. Click the **Crop** button to turn it off.

  • To crop us-ing units, double-click the picture and click the **Picture** tab. Use the respective spinner to set how much to remove from a side. Click **OK** when finished.

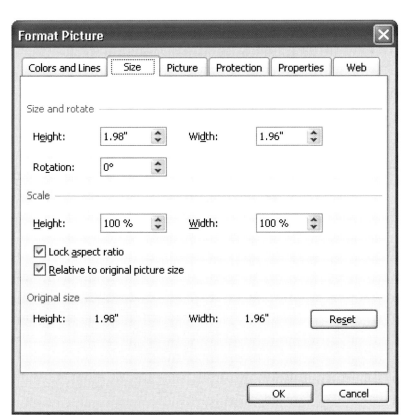

Figure 7- 13: The Format dialog box Size tab lets you precisely size a graphic by units of measurement or by scaling based on percentage

POSITIONING GRAPHICS

While graphics can be positioned by simply dragging them, Excel also provides a number of other techniques that help you adjust where a graphic is in relation to other graphics and objects as well as how graphics move in relation to cells on the worksheet.

MOVE GRAPHICS INCREMENTALLY

Select the graphic or group, press and hold **CTRL**, and press the arrow key in the direction you want to move.

–Or–

Open **Draw** on the Drawing toolbar, point at **Nudge**, and click the direction you want the graphic moved.

RE-POSITION THE ORDER OF STACKED GRAPHICS

You can stack graphics by simply dragging one on top of another. To re-position the order of the stack, right-click the graphic you want to change, point at **Order**, and click:

- **Bring To Front**, to move the graphic to the top of the stack
- **Send To Back**, to move the graphic to the bottom of the stack
- **Bring Forward**, to move the graphic up one level (same as Bring To Front if there are only two graphics in the stack)
- **Send Backward**, to move the graphic up down level (same as Send To Back if there are only two graphics in the stack)

Continued...

Combine Graphics by Grouping

You can combine graphics for any number of reasons, but you typically work with multiple graphics to build a more complex drawing. To prevent losing the positioning, sizing, and other characteristics of these components, you can group them so that they are treated as one graphic.

GROUP GRAPHICS

1. Select the graphics to be grouped by clicking the first graphic and then pressing and holding **SHIFT** while selecting the other graphics.
2. Point at **Draw** on the Drawing toolbar and click **Group**, or right-click one of the selected graphics, point at **Grouping**, and click **Group**. A single set of selection handles surrounds the perimeter of the graphics. Coloring, positioning, sizing, and other actions now affect the graphics as a group instead of individually.

UNGROUP GRAPHICS

To separate a group into individual graphics, select the group, point at **Draw** on the Drawing toolbar, and click **Ungroup**, or right-click the group, point at **Grouping**, and click **Ungroup**.

RE-COMBINE A GROUP AFTER UNGROUPING

After making a modification to a graphic that was part of a group, you don't have to re-select each component graphic to reestablish the group. Select any graphic that was in the group, point at **Draw** on the Drawing toolbar, and click **Regroup**, or right-click a member graphic, point at **Grouping**, and click **Regroup**.

Create a Mirrored Image

1. Select the graphic you want to be half of the mirrored image, click **Copy**, and click **Paste**. A second copy of the image is place on top of the original and is selected.

2. Open **Draw**, point at **Rotate Or Flip**, and click **Flip Horizontal** or **Flip Vertical**, depending on how you want the image to look.

3. Press **SHIFT** and select the original graphic. Both graphics should be selected.

4. Open **Draw**, point at **Align Or Distribute**, and click an applicable alignment to make the graphics even.

5. Select only the top graphic, press and hold **CTRL** and click/press the applicable arrow key to nudge the graphic into a mirrored position.

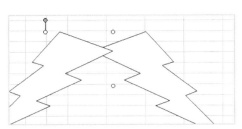

Keep Changes Intact

You can prevent someone, including yourself, from make inadvertent changes to graphics you might have spent considerable time creating.

1. Verify the worksheet is *protected* (see Chapter 9).

2. Double-click the graphic, and click the **Protection** tab in the Format dialog box.

3. Verify the **Locked** check box is selected, and click **OK**.

Chapter 8
Managing Data

Excel, as you've seen in other chapters, "excels" at calculating and displaying data. This chapter shows you how to manage, organize, and acquire data. In this chapter, you will learn how to set up a properly constructed list, enter data from a simple form, organize data by sorting, and retrieve just the data you want by setting up filters, acquire data from external sources, and ensure added data meets criteria you establish.

Build Lists

Excel provides the ability to work with data in *lists*. Lists, like databases, consist of columns of similar data—the names of all the salespeople in a company, for example. Each salesperson covers a certain region, so this list would also need a Territory column. Each salesperson has a cell phone number; each has projected sales targets and actual sales, and so forth. You could say each salesperson has a collection of information pertaining to just them. In an Excel list, each row in the worksheet contains this collection of unique data—unique in the sense that while two or more salespeople might call Washington their Territory, each row contains data for only one salesperson.

Create a List

The new List command in Excel 2003 makes creating a list easier than ever. However, before you designate a range of data to be a list you might want to consider reorganizing your data to better work with list features:

- **Column headings** (or *labels*) should be formatted differently than the data so Excel can more easily differentiate one from the other. Data in a column should be similar. Avoid mixing dates and other number formats with text.

- **Clean the worksheet** by eliminating any blank rows or columns within the range and removing extra spaces in cells.

- **Display all data** by unhiding any rows or columns you might have hidden. Hidden data can be inadvertently deleted.

- **Place values to be totaled** in the rightmost column. Excel's Total Row feature creates a total row which you can toggle off or on when it recognizes data that can be summed in the last column.

1. Open **Data**, point at **List**, and click **Create List**. The Create List dialog box opens showing which cells it thinks you want to include in the list. To change the range, click the **Collapse Dialog** button to see more of the worksheet, select the range, and click the **Expand Dialog** button to return to the Create List dialog box.

2. Verify the **My List Has Header**s (column headings—your list should have them) check box is selected, and click **OK**.

3. Click inside the selected data. The list is surrounded by a dark blue border, AutoFilter arrows are added to the column headings (see "Create an AutoFilter" later in the chapter for information on using filters), and the List toolbar displays, as shown in Figure 8-1.

QUICKSTEPS

ADDING ROWS AND COLUMNS TO A LIST

ADD ROWS TO THE END OF THE LIST

- Click the cell that contains the blue add-new-row asterisk. When you complete the entry, the asterisk moves to the next row below.

–Or–

- Type in an empty row that is adjacent to the end of the list. The list will "annex" the row unless the last row is empty or the last row is a total row.

–Or–

- Drag the lower-right corner of the list downward over the rows you want to add.

ADD COLUMNS TO THE SIDES OF A LIST

- Type in an empty column that is adjacent to the list. The list will "annex" the column.

–Or–

- Drag the lower-right corner of the list to the right over the columns you want to add.

ADD ROWS AND COLUMNS WITHIN A LIST

1. Click in the column to the right of or in the row below where you want to add more cells.

2. Open **List** on the List toolbar, point at **Insert**, and depending on where you want the cells added, click **Row** or **Column**.

–Or–

1. Right-click the column to the right of or the row below where you want to add more cells.

2. Point at **Insert** and click **Row** or **Column**, depending on where you want the cells added.

Continued…

AutoFilter arrows, let you quickly sort and filter data in a column

Dark blue border, surrounds a list when the active cell is in the list

List toolbar, provides several list-related options

Add-new-row asterisk, identifies where you can add data to the end of your list

Figure 8-1: You can identify data as being a list by the blue border that surrounds it

Enter and Manage Data Using a Form

You can enter data into a list using the same methods described earlier in this book, such as by typing in the cell or by using the Formula bar. Lists offer an alternate way to enter data by using a form that lets you enter one row (record) of data at a time.

1. Click a cell in the list.

2. Open **Data** and click **Form**. A dialog box with the worksheet name as its title opens with the first record's data displayed, as shown in Figure 8-2.

ADD A NEW RECORD

1. Click the **New** button.

2. Type data in each text box, pressing **TAB** between each field (column) name.

3. Press **ENTER** to complete the entry. The data is added to the bottom of the list as a new row.

DELETE A RECORD

1. Locate the record to be deleted. (See the Quick-Steps "Locating Data Using a Form.")

2. Click the **Delete** button, and click **OK** to confirm the deletion as permanent.

MODIFY DATA

1. Locate the record that contains the data to be modified. (See the QuickSteps "Locating Data Using a Form.")

2. Edit the data by selecting the text and numbers to be changed and typing the new information.

3. Press **ENTER** when you are finished changing data in the displayed record.

TIP

If rows or columns are not added to a list when you drag the lower-right corner of a selected list over them, open **Tools**, select **AutoCorrect Options**, and click the **AutoFormat As You Type** tab. Select the **Include New Rows And Columns In List** check box.

TIP

You can undo any changes you make to the current record in the form by pressing the **Restore** button before you press ENTER.

NOTE

The form described in this section is referred to as a *data entry* form. You can also use Excel to create common business forms that are printed or used on the Web. Several examples are available on your computer, and more are located on the Office Online web site. Open **File** and click **New**. In the New Workbook task pane, under Templates, select **On My Computer**. The Templates dialog box opens. The Spreadsheet Solutions tab displays forms that can be used as is or can be modified to your unique needs. Click **Templates On Office Online** to see more samples.

Figure 8-2: Data can be managed in a list by using a form that displays the column/field names

Add a Total Row

Excel provides a nifty feature that sums the last column in a list and automatically creates a Total row at the bottom of the list. The Total Row lets you perform other calculations on any of the columns in the list.

SUM THE LAST COLUMN

1. Select a cell in the list to display the List toolbar.

2. Click **Toggle Total Row**. The rightmost column is summed,  and a new row with the word Total in the leftmost cell is added below the add-new-row asterisk, as shown in Figure 8-3.

3. To remove the Total row, simply click the **Toggle Total Row** button again.

CALCULATE VALUES IN A COLUMN

1. Click the list to display the List toolbar, and click the **Toggle Total Row** button to turn on that feature.

2. In the Total row at the bottom of the list, click the cell at the bottom of a column whose values you want to calculate. A down  arrow appears to the right of the cell.

3. Click the down arrow, and select the calculation you want performed (see Figure 8-3). The result is displayed in the cell.

4. Click the **Toggle Total Row** button to remove the Total row and calculated result.

Remove a List

1. Select a cell in the list.

2. In the List toolbar, click the **List** down arrow and select **Convert To Range**. Click **Yes** to confirm you want to convert the list to a normal range.

LOCATING DATA USING A FORM *(Continued)*

LOCATE BY ENTERING CRITERIA

1. Click the **Criteria** button. The fields are cleared of data, and the command buttons are revised.

2. Type the search criteria in the applicable field's text box. For example, to find:

   - A **name** such as a person or company, type the name

   - A **value**, type the number, or use comparison operators such as greater than (>) and the number or less than (<) and the number

   - An entry based on **more than one criteria**, type the criteria in each applicable text box

3. Click **Find Next** or **Find Prev**, depending on which part of the list you want searched. Click **Close** when finished, or click **Form** to return to data entry.

USE WILDCARDS IN CRITERIA

You can use *wildcard* comparison criteria to help you find data.

- Type an asterisk (*****) as a placeholder for any number of missing characters. For example, typing *son finds Robinson, Dobson, and bison.

- Type a question mark (**?**) as a placeholder for a single character. For example, typing Jo?n finds John and Joan.

- Type a tilde (**~**) before an asterisk, question mark, or tilde to find words or phrases containing any of those three characters. For example, typing msdos~~ finds msdos~.

Figure 8-3: Turning on the Toggle Total Row button on the List toolbar sums the numbers in the rightmost column and provides cells to calculate column values

Clicking Toggle Total Row...

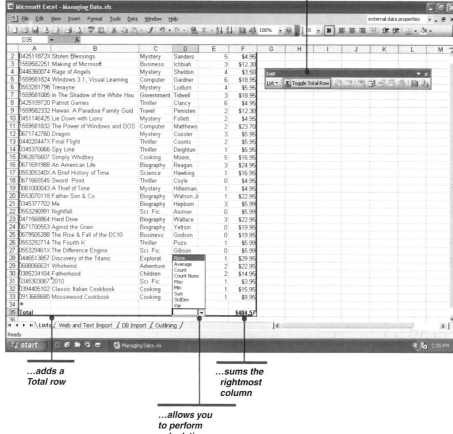

...adds a Total row

...sums the rightmost column

...allows you to perform calculations on the column values

8

Figure 8-4: The Data Validation dialog box provides comparison criteria you can use to establish conditions for data entry

	A	B	C	D	E	F
1	ISBN	Title	Category	Author	OnHand	Price
2	042511872X	Stolen Blessings	Mystery	Sanders	5	$4.95
3	1559582251	Making of Microsoft	Business	Ichbiah	3	$12.30
4	0446360074	Rage of Angels	Mystery	Sheldon	4	$3.50
5	1559581824	Windows 3.1, Visual Learning	Computer	Gardner	6	$18.95
6	0553281798	Trevayne	Mystery	Ludlum	4	$5.95
7	1559581085	In The Shadow of the White Hou	Government	Tidwell	3	$18.95
8	0425109720	Patriot Games	Thriller	Clancy	4	$4.95
9	1559582332	Hawaii: A Paradise Family Guid	Travel	Penisten	2	$12.30
10	0451146425	Lie Down with Lions	Mystery	Follett	2	$4.95
11	1559581832	The Power of Windows and DOS	Computer	Matthews	2	$23.70
12	0671742760	Dragon	Mystery	Cussler	3	$5.95
13	044020447X	Final Flight	Thriller	Coonts	2	$5.95
14	0345370066	Spy Line	Thriller	Deightun	1	$5.95
15	0962876607	Simply Whidbey	Cooking	Moore,	5	$16.95
16	0671691988	An American Life	Biography	Reagan	3	$24.95
17	055305340X	A Brief History of Time	Science	Hawking	1	$16.95
18	0671665545	Sword Point	Thriller	Coyle	0	$4.95
19	0061000043	A Thief of Time	Mystery	Hillerman	1	$4.95
20	0553070118	Father Son & Co.	Biography	Watson Jr	1	$22.95
21	0345377702	Me	Biography	Hepburn	2	$5.99
22	0553290991	Nightfall	Sci. Fic.	Asimov	0	$5.99
23	0471568864	Hard Drive	Biography	Wallace	3	$22.95
24	0671700553	Aginst the Grain	Biography	Yeltsin	0	$19.95
25	0679505288	The Rise & Fall of the DC10	Business	Godson	0	$19.95
26	0553292714	The Fourth K	Thriller	Puzo	1	$5.99
27	055329461X	The Difference Engine	Sci. Fic.	Gibson	0	$5.99
28	0446513857	Discovery of the Titanic	Explorat.	Ballard	1	$29.95
29	0688066631	Whirlwind	Adventure	Clavell	2	$22.95
30	0385234104	Fatherhood	Children	Cosby	2	$14.95
31	0345303067	2010	Sci. Fic.	Clarke	1	$3.95
32	0394405102	Classic Italian Cookbook	Cooking	Hazan	1	$15.95
33	0913668680	Moosewood Cookbook	Cooking	Katzen	1	$9.95
34	*					

Figure 8-5: Cells that have validation applied are highlighted

Validate Data

To prevent data entry errors, you can set validation criteria. Excel checks the entered data against the criteria you set and disallows the entry if the validation conditions are not met. You can use data validation in any cell on the worksheet; however; due to the quantity of data typically entered in a list, using data validation in lists is highly recommended.

Additionally, you can choose to have Excel display a message when a user selects a validated cell, and you can choose to have Excel display an error alert when an attempt is made to enter invalid data in the cell.

CREATE A VALIDATION

1. Select the cells you want validated. Typically, you would select a column. Do not select column or row headings, since they are probably formatted as text and might cause compatibility problems with numbered data.

2. Open **Data** and click **Validation**. The Data Validation dialog box opens with the Settings tab displayed, as shown in Figure 8-4.

3. Click the **Allow** down arrow, and select the validation criteria to use.

4. Click the **Data** down arrow, and select the comparison operator to use.

5. Type minimum/starting and maximum/ending values in the applicable text boxes, or locate them on the worksheet using the **Collapse Dialog** button. If using values on the worksheet, click the **Expand Dialog** button to return to the dialog box.

6. Click **OK** to apply the validation.

FIND VALIDATED DATA

1. Open **Edit**, select **Go To**, and click **Special**.

2. In the Go To Special dialog box, select **Data Validation** and click **All**.

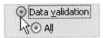

3. Click **OK**. All validated data is selected, as shown in Figure 8-5.

TIP

To find other occurrences of the validation in a cell, select the cell before you open the Go To dialog box. In the Go To Special dialog box, choose **Same** under Data Validation. When you click OK, only the cells whose validation matches the selected cell will be highlighted.

TIP

You can create a message to appear when *any* cell is selected, not just those that have validation conditions applied—although Comments are typically used for that purpose. See Chapter 3 for information on adding Comments to a cell.

REMOVE VALIDATION CRITERIA

1. Select the cell(s) whose validation you want to remove. See "Find Validated Data" to help you locate the validated cells.

2. Open **Data** and click **Validation**.

3. If you are prompted to erase the current validation settings, click **OK** and then click **Cancel** in the Data Validation dialog box.

   –Or–

   In the Data Validation dialog box Settings tab, click **Clear All**, and then click **OK**.

4. Verify the validation was removed by doing the procedures in "Find Validated Data."

CREATE A DATA ENTRY MESSAGE

You can forestall data entry mistakes by providing a message, similar to a ScreenTip, with information about a selected cell.

1. Set up a validation. See "Create a Validation."

2. Open **Data**, select **Validation**, and click the **Input Message** tab.

3. Verify that the **Show Input Message When Cell Is Selected** check box is selected.

☑ Show input message when cell is selected

4. Type a title for the message and the message itself in their respective text boxes.

5. Click **OK** when finished. When a user selects a cell to enter data, a ScreenTip-type message will be displayed with the text you provided.

CREATE AN ERROR MESSAGE

When you (or anyone else!) try to add data that doesn't meet a cell's validation criteria, Excel returns a generic message box that informs you of your transgression. You can modify the type of alert that is displayed and the text that appears.

1. Set up a validation. See "Create a Validation."

2. Open **Data**, select **Validation**, and click the **Error Alert** tab.

3. Verify that the **Show Error Alert After Invalid Data Is Entered** check box is selected.

4. Open the **Style** drop-down list box, and select the severity of the alert. The alert's associated icon is displayed below the selected style.

5. Type a title for the alert and the message itself in their respective text boxes.

6. Click **OK** when finished. When a user tries to complete an entry with data that doesn't meet the validation criteria, the alert you created will pop up, as shown in Figure 8-6.

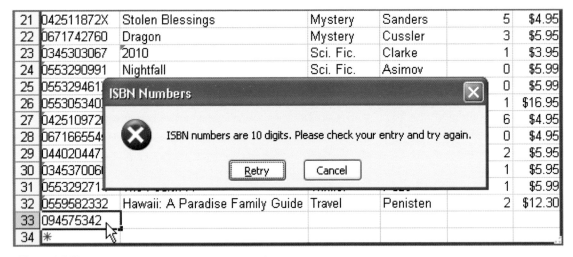

Figure 8-6: You can create custom error messages to alert users that they are trying to enter invalid data

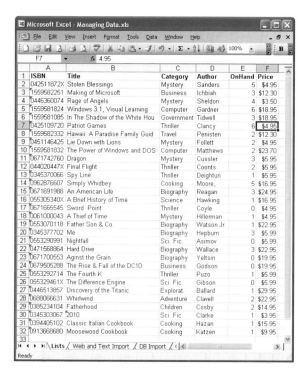

Figure 8-7: Click a cell anywhere in the range to start the
process of sorting data

Organize Data

Data in a worksheet is often entered in a manner that doesn't lend itself to being
viewed or to being able to find specific data that you want. Excel provides
several tools to assist you in organizing your data without permanently
changing the overall structure of the worksheet. You can sort data on
any column in ascending or descending order, filter data to view just the
information you want to see, and outline data to streamline what you see.

Sort Data by Columns

You sort data in ascending or descending order according to the values in one
or more columns. All data in the range is realigned so that the data in each row
remains the same, even though the row might be placed in a different order
than it was originally. You can also sort on dates and days of week, and use
values listed by rows instead of columns.

SORT BY A SINGLE COLUMN

1. Click a cell in the column you want to sort the range by.

2. On the Standard toolbar, either:

   ● Click **Sort Ascending** to sort from smaller to larger numbers and from A to
     Z. (See the Note on sort orders at the end of this section.)

   –Or–

   ● Click **Sort Descending** to sort from larger to smaller numbers and from Z to A.

SORT BY MULTIPLE COLUMNS

1. Click a cell in the range you want to sort, as shown in Figure 8-7.

2. Open **Data** and click **Sort**. The Sort dialog box opens.

3. In the My Data Range Has area, select whether your range
   has column headings or not.

4. Open the **Sort By** drop-down list box, select the column of
   primary importance in determining the sort order, and click
   Ascending or **Descending**.

TIP

You can sort by *four* columns, but you have to "trick"
Excel a bit by doing the sort in two steps. First, sort on
the least specific column in the Sort dialog box, and click
OK. Next, complete a second sort in the Sort dialog box
as you normally would, from the most to the least specific
column, utilizing the three Sort By drop-down list boxes.
Click **OK** to close the Sort dialog box a second time.

NOTE

If you try to sort a range that includes numbers formatted as text, you will see a warning dialog box that lets you choose how you want to handle the sort.

NOTE

Sorting in Excel is determined by a specified *sort order*. For example, numbers in an ascending sort are sorted before letters; combined number and letter (*alphanumeric*) values are sorted next, logical values with False, then logical values with True; error values; and finally, any blanks.

5. Open the first **Then By** drop-down list box, select the column you want to base the sort on that is of secondary importance, and click **Ascending** or **Descending**.

6. Repeat, if necessary, for the third Then By drop-down list box.

7. Click **OK**. The data is sorted based on your sorting criteria. See Figure 8-8.

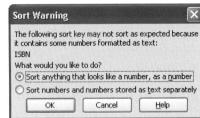

Sort Data by Rows

1. Click a cell in the range you want to sort. (The range cannot be an Excel-defined list.)

2. Open **Data** and click **Sort**. The Sort dialog box opens.

3. Click **Options**. The Sort Options dialog box opens.

4. In the Orientation area, click **Sort Left To Right**. Click **OK**.

5. Open the **Sort By** drop-down list box, select the row of primary importance in determining the sort order, and click **Ascending** or **Descending**.

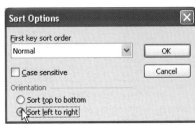

6. Repeat, if necessary, for the first and second Then By drop-down list boxes.

7. Click **OK**.

Secondary sort, on Category   Third sort, on Author   Primary sort, on Price

	ISBN	Title	Category	Author	OnHand	Price
2	0446360074	Rage of Angels	Mystery	Sheldon	4	$3.50
3	0345303067	2010	Sci. Fic.	Clarke	1	$3.95
4	0451146425	Lie Down with Lions	Mystery	Follett	2	$4.95
5	0061000043	A Thief of Time	Mystery	Hillerman	1	$4.95
6	042511872X	Stolen Blessings	Mystery	Sanders	5	$4.95
7	0425109720	Patriot Games	Thriller	Clancy	6	$4.95
8	0671665545	Sword Point	Thriller	Coyle	0	$4.95
9	0671742760	Dragon	Mystery	Cussler	3	$5.95
10	044020447X	Final Flight	Thriller	Coonts	2	$5.95
11	0345370066	Spy Line	Thriller	Deighton	1	$5.95
12	0345377702	Me	Biography	Hepburn	3	$5.99
13	0553290991	Nightfall	Sci. Fic.	Asimov	0	$5.99
14	055329461X	The Difference Engine	Sci. Fic.	Gibson	0	$5.99
15	0553292714	The Fourth K	Thriller	Puzo	1	$5.99
16	0913668680	Moosewood Cookbook	Cooking	Katzen	1	$9.95
17	1559582251	Making of Microsoft	Business	Ichbiah	3	$12.30
18	1559582332	Hawaii: A Paradise Family Guid	Travel	Penisten	2	$12.30
19	0385234104	Fatherhood	Children	Cosby	2	$14.95
20	0394405102	Classic Italian Cookbook	Cooking	Hazan	1	$15.95
21	0962876607	Simply Whidbey	Cooking	Moore,	5	$16.95
22	055305340X	A Brief History of Time	Science	Hawking	1	$16.95
23	1559581824	Windows 3.1, Visual Learning	Computer	Gardner	6	$18.95
24	1559581085	In The Shadow of the White Hou	Government	Tidwell	3	$18.95
25	0671700553	Aginst the Grain	Biography	Yeltsin	0	$19.95
26	0679505288	The Rise & Fall of the DC10	Business	Godson	0	$19.95
27	0688066631	Whirlwind	Adventure	Clavell	2	$22.95
28	0471568864	Hard Drive	Biography	Wallace	3	$22.95
29	0553070118	Father Son & Co.	Biography	Watson Jr.	1	$22.95
30	1559581832	The Power of Windows and DOS	Computer	Matthews	2	$23.70
31	0671691988	An American Life	Biography	Reagan	3	$24.95
32	0446513857	Discovery of the Titanic	Explorat.	Ballard	1	$29.95

Figure 8-8: Compare the data shown in Figure 8-7 to how the data appears here after being sorted by three columns

Create an AutoFilter

Filtering data allows you to quickly dismiss potentially thousands of rows (records) of data that you don't need at the moment so that only those rows of data that you want to see are displayed. The quickest and easiest way to filter data is to have Excel add AutoFilter drop-down lists to your column headings.

1. Click a cell in the range where you want to filter data.

2. Open **Data**, point at **Filters**, and click **AutoFilter**. Down arrows are added to the right of each column heading.

3. Click the AutoFilter down arrow in the column that contains the values you want to apply a filter to.

C	D	E	F
Category ▼	Author ▼	OnHar ▼	Pric ▼
Mystery	Sheldon	4	$3.50

4. Decide what you want to filter, and follow the appropriate steps below.

FILTER ON COLUMN VALUES

Click the value from the AutoFilter list.

FILTER ON SPECIFIC TEXT

1. Click **Custom** in the AutoFilter list.

2. In the Custom AutoFilter dialog box, open the first drop-down list box, and select a comparison operator.

3. Type the text you want to filter on in the combo box.

4. Click **And** or **Or** to add another condition to the filter, using wildcards to represent single or multiple characters.

5. Click **OK**.

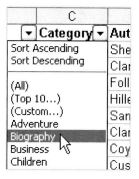

FILTER FOR EMPTY OR FILLED CELLS

The Blanks and NoBlanks options are only displayed if the column has at least one blank cell.

- Click **Blanks** to display rows that have a blank cell in the column.

    –Or–

- Click **NonBlanks** to display just rows that contain data.

FILTER FOR THE TOP/BOTTOM VALUES

1. In a column of numeric values, click **Top 10...** The Top 10 Auto-Filter dialog box opens.

2. Select whether to display the Top or Bottom values, how many values to display, and whether to show by items or by percent.

3. Click **OK**.

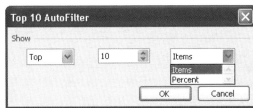

Outline Data Automatically

You can display only summary rows and columns by outlining a range and hiding the details. The mechanics of creating the automatic outline involve just a few clicks; however, there are a few things you should do to your data in advance of applying an automatic outline:

- **Column headings** should be in the first row if you are outlining by row; **row headings** should be in the first column if you are outlining by column.
- **Similar data** should be in the columns or rows you are performing the outline on, and the data must be set up as a hierarchical summary.
- **Blank rows or columns** should be removed.
- **Sort the data** to get it into the groupings you want.
- **Create total or summary rows and columns** that sum the detail rows above or the detail columns to the left or right.

TIP

The AutoFilter drop-down list shows only the first *1000* unique values!

QUICKSTEPS

REMOVING FILTERS

REMOVE A FILTER FROM A COLUMN

1. Open the **AutoFilter menu** by clicking the down arrow next to the column heading.

2. Click **(All)**.

REMOVE FILTERS FROM ALL COLUMNS IN A RANGE OR LIST

Open **Data**, point at **Filter**, and click **Show All**.

REMOVE THE AUTOFILTER DOWN ARROWS

Open **Data**, point at **Filters**, and click **AutoFilter** to turn off the toggle.

When you are ready to outline your data:

1. Click a cell in the range you want to outline.

2. Open **Data**, point at **Group And Outline**, and click **Auto Outline**. An outlining bar and outlining symbols are either added across the column headers and down the row headers, as shown in Figure 8-9, or across just one of the headers—depending on the structure of your data. See the QuickSteps "Using Outlines" for ways to manipulate your data.

Outline Data by Grouping

Grouping data allows you to create an outline of your data by selecting rows and columns that can be collapsed and hidden. You generally use this manual method of outlining when your data doesn't have the summary rows or columns used by the automatic outlining feature to recognize where to hide details.

1. Select the first set of rows or columns you want to be able to collapse and expand.

2. Open **Data**, point at **Group And Outline**, and click **Group**. An outlining bar is added to the left of the row headers or above the column headers, depending on whether rows or columns were selected.

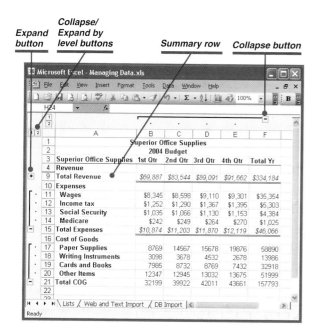

3. Repeat Steps 1 and 2 for as many sets of rows or columns you want to include in the outline.

Add Styles to an Outline

Excel can recognize summary rows and columns and can add styling to differentiate them from other data.

1. Expand the outline to show any collapsed rows or columns.

2. Select the range of cells, including detail data and summary rows or columns, where you want to apply styling.

3. Open **Data**, point at **Group And Outline**, and click **Settings**.

Expand *button*

Collapse/ Expand by level buttons

Summary row

Collapse button

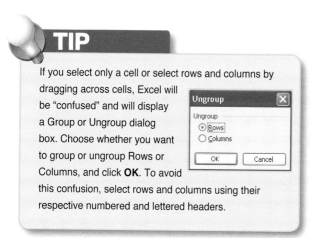

Figure 8-9: Excel provides outlining tools to collapse and expand data by row or column

TIP

If you select only a cell or select rows and columns by dragging across cells, Excel will be "confused" and will display a Group or Ungroup dialog box. Choose whether you want to group or ungroup Rows or Columns, and click **OK**. To avoid this confusion, select rows and columns using their respective numbered and lettered headers.

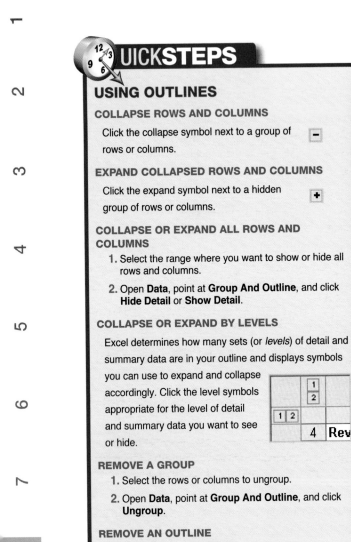

QUICKSTEPS

USING OUTLINES

COLLAPSE ROWS AND COLUMNS

Click the collapse symbol next to a group of rows or columns.

EXPAND COLLAPSED ROWS AND COLUMNS

Click the expand symbol next to a hidden group of rows or columns.

COLLAPSE OR EXPAND ALL ROWS AND COLUMNS

1. Select the range where you want to show or hide all rows and columns.

2. Open **Data**, point at **Group And Outline**, and click **Hide Detail** or **Show Detail**.

COLLAPSE OR EXPAND BY LEVELS

Excel determines how many sets (or *levels*) of detail and summary data are in your outline and displays symbols you can use to expand and collapse accordingly. Click the level symbols appropriate for the level of detail and summary data you want to see or hide.

REMOVE A GROUP

1. Select the rows or columns to ungroup.

2. Open **Data**, point at **Group And Outline**, and click **Ungroup**.

REMOVE AN OUTLINE

1. Select a cell in the outline.

2. Open **Data**, point at **Group And Outline**, and click **Clear Outline**.

4. In the Settings dialog box, select the **Automatic Styles** check box, and click **Apply Styles**. Bolding is applied to summary rows and/or columns.

	16	Cost of Goods					
·	17	Paper Supplies	$8,769	$14,567	$15,678	$19,876	$58,890
·	18	Writing Instruments	$3,098	$3,678	$4,532	$2,678	$13,986
·	19	Cards and Books	$7,985	$8,732	$8,769	$7,432	$32,918
·	20	Other Items	$12,347	$12,945	$13,032	$13,675	$51,999
	21	Total COG	$32,199	$39,922	$42,011	$43,661	$157,793

Acquire Data

In addition to typing data directly onto a worksheet or entering data by using a form—both of which are time consuming and prone to error—you can import data from an external source into Excel. Once the data is "safely" on an Excel worksheet, you have all the tools and features this book describes to format, organize, analyze, or otherwise whip the data into the shape you want. You can import data from several *data sources*, including text files, the Web, and databases. Data sources include the *links* to source data and are comprised of the source data itself, information needed to locate the data (or database server), and information needed to access the data, such as user names and passwords.

Convert Text to Data

Text files are files with file extensions such as TXT and CSV (comma-separated values) that can be formatted using commas, spaces, tabs, and other separators to organize data. Though the data might not appear to be structured, as shown in Figure 8-10, Excel can correctly place the data into columns and rows as long as the data is separated in a consistent and recognizable format.

1. Select the cell into which you want to place the beginning of the range of imported data.

2. Open **Data**, point at **Import External Data**, and click **Import Data**.

NOTE

Connecting to external data sources to import data can quickly become an involved and complicated endeavor. System and database administrators might need to get involved to ensure that you have the proper authorization to access the network, the servers involved, and the data itself. If you need to connect to data beyond the three types described in this section, contact your technical support resources.

Figure 8-10: Text files might look like a jumble of unrelated data, but Excel can "see through" the clutter and correctly place it in rows and columns on a worksheet

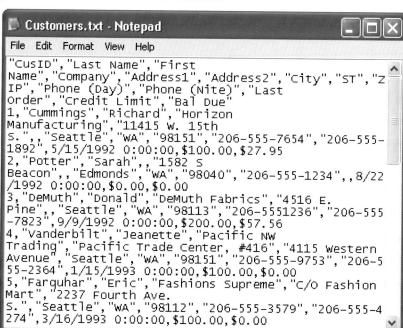

3. In the Select Data Source dialog box, open the **Files Of Type** drop-down list box, and select **Text Files**. Locate and select the text file, and click **Open**. Step 1 of the Text Import Wizard opens.

4. Preview the file in the lower half of the dialog box. If all appears to be in order, Excel has done a good job so far. If needed, make the following choices or decisions, which immediately change the preview:

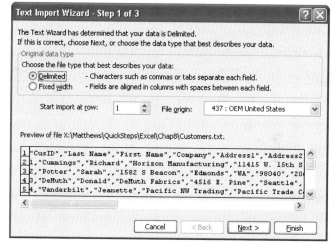

- Determine if the file is delimited (separated) by characters or if it is a fixed width. You can further refine your choice in Step 2 of the wizard.

- Decide from where in the text file you want to start importing data. You may not want the headings row if the file contains one. In that case, you would change the Start Import At Row spinner to 2.

- Choose a File Origin that matches the text language used in the file.

5. Click **Next** or—if you feel "lucky"—click **Finish**. (You can always delete and start again).

6. Step 2 of the wizard lets you fine tune the delimiter used or set field widths (depending on your choice in Step 1) and preview how the changes align the data. Experiment with the delimiter option or column widths and see which makes the preview most representative of how you want the data organized. Click **Next** or **Finish**.

1

2

3

4

5

6

7

8

9

10

7. Step 3 of the wizard lets you apply data formats on a column-by-column basis. You can also format the columns in the worksheet. Click **Finish**.

8. Verify where you want the data placed—either in the current worksheet or in a new worksheet. Make your choice and click **OK**. The data is displayed in Excel as shown in Figure 8-11.

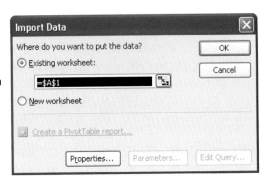

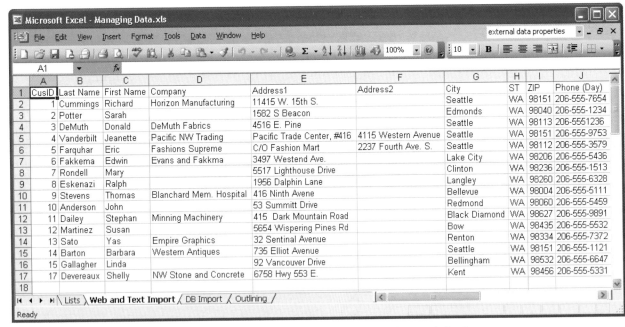

Figure 8-11: Data imported from a text file is indistinguishable from other data in a worksheet

Add All Data from an Access Table

You can add data from an Access database by choosing from a list of tables that the database contains.

1. Select the cell into which you want to place the beginning of the range of imported data.

2. Open **Data**, point at **Import External Data**, and click **Import Data**.

3. In the Select Data Source dialog box, locate and select the Access database that contains the table of data you want. Click **Open**.

4. In the Select Table dialog box, select the table you want and click **OK**.

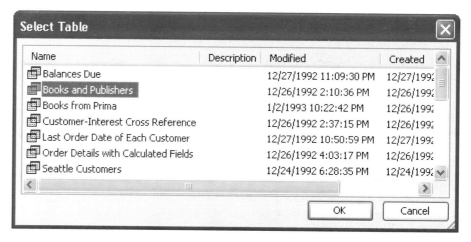

5. In the Import Data dialog box, verify where you want the data placed—either in the current worksheet or in a new worksheet. Make your choice and click **OK**.

Add Selective Data from an Access Table

You can be more selective in what data you import by creating a *query*. A query is a set of parameters that include the connection information, the database object(s) that is to be searched, and criteria that specifies any filtering or sorting. Queries are created in Microsoft Query, an add-in program that you might need to install.

INSTALL MICROSOFT QUERY

1. Open **Data**, point at **Import External Data**, and click **New Database Query**.

2. If you do not have Microsoft Query installed, you will see a message box informing you of that and giving you the opportunity to install it. Click **Yes**. You might need your Office CD or path to a network installation location to complete the installation.

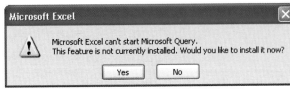

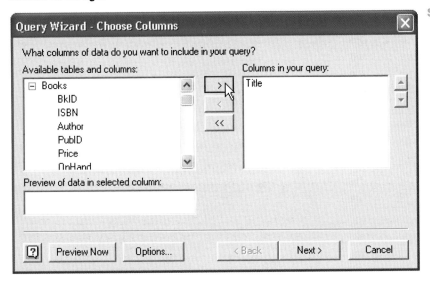

Figure 8-12: Include columns in your query by moving the available columns from the list box on the left to the list box on the right

Query Wizard - Choose Columns

What columns of data do you want to include in your query?

Available tables and columns:

- ☐ Books
  - BkID
  - ISBN
  - Author
  - PubID
  - Price
  - OnHand

Columns in your query:

- Title

Preview of data in selected column:

? | Preview Now | Options... | < Back | Next > | Cancel

SET UP A QUERY USING A WIZARD

1. Open **Data**, point at **Import External Data**, and click **New Database Query**.

2. In the Choose Data Source dialog box Databases tab, select **MS Access Database**, and ensure the **Use The Query Wizard To Create/Edit Queries** check box is selected. Click **OK**.

   ☑ Use the Query Wizard to create/edit queries

3. In the Select Database dialog box, locate and select the Access database you want, and click **OK**. The Query Wizard opens.

4. In the Query Wizard-Choose Columns dialog box, click the plus (+) sign next to the table you want to search to display its columns. The plus sign will change to a minus (-) after you open it.

5. Select a column whose data you want to import into Excel, and then click the right-pointing button in the center of the dialog box to move the column to the Columns In Your Query, as shown in Figure 8-12. Repeat for any other columns you want to import into Excel. Change the order of the columns by selecting a column name and clicking the up and down arrows on the right. Then either:

- Click **Next** twice and then click **Finish** to import all the data in your selected columns.

  –Or–

- Click **Next** to continue the wizard and create filtering and sorting criteria.

TIP

If you are unsure of the data in a column in the Query Wizard-Choose Columns dialog box, click **Preview Now,** and scroll through the Preview Of Data In Selected Column text box before you move the column to the list box on the right.

NOTE

You do not have to use a wizard to create a query. To create a query from the Microsoft Query window, deselect the **Use The Query Wizard To Create/Edit Queries** check box in the Choose Data Source dialog box. (To do this, open **Data**, point at **Import External Data**, and click **New Database Query**.) Click **OK**, and then select the database, add tables, and use the menu and toolbar options to create the query. Unless you are familiar with working with databases and creating queries, I suggest you use the wizard!

6. In the Query Wizard-Filter Data dialog box, create a filter that specifies what rows are included in the query by selecting a Column To Filter and opening the first comparison drop-down list box. Select the comparison operator and then the value or values that will satisfy the filter. Click **Next**.

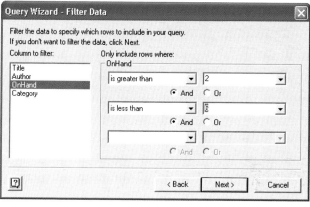

7. In the Query Wizard-Sort Order dialog box, choose how to sort the query results. Click **Next**.

8. In the Query Wizard-Finish dialog box, leave the default option **Return Data To Microsoft Office Excel** selected and either:

- Click **Finish**.

  –Or–

- If you might want to repeat the query, click **Save Query**. In the Save As dialog box, name the query, click **Save**, and then click **Finish**.

9. Verify where you want the data placed—either in the current worksheet or in a new worksheet. Make your choice and click **OK**. The results of your query are displayed in Excel, as shown in Figure 8-13.

Figure 8-13: The filtered results of a query display only the data you ask for

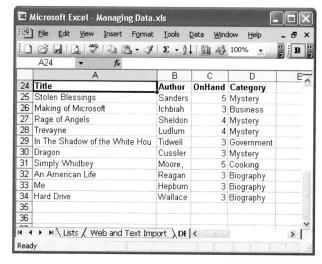

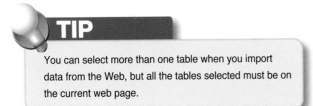

TIP

You can select more than one table when you import data from the Web, but all the tables selected must be on the current web page.

Get Data from the Web

More and more data is being offered on the web sites of companies and individuals. In the past, you were limited to copying and pasting, which tended to provide inconsistent formatting and, often, just plain strange results. Excel now lets you select what tables of data you want from a web page and import them in a few clicks.

1. Select the cell into which you want to place the beginning of the range of imported data.

2. Open **Data**, point at **Import External Data**, and click **New Web Query**.

3. In the New Web Query dialog box, shown in Figure 8-14, type the address of the web site from which you want to retrieve data and then navigate to the page where the data is located.

4. Click the table selection arrow in the upper-leftmost corner of each table whose data you want. The arrow changes to a check mark when selected.

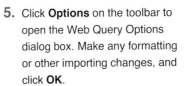

5. Click **Options** on the toolbar to open the Web Query Options dialog box. Make any formatting or other importing changes, and click **OK**.

6. Click **Import**. Verify where you want the data placed—either in the current worksheet or in a new worksheet. Make your choice and click **OK**. The data is displayed in Excel.

Figure 8-14: The New Web Query dialog box displays a web page from where you can select tables of data to import into Excel

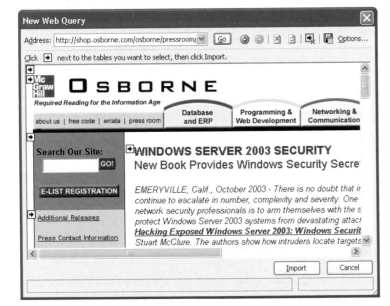

Change External Data

Data you import onto a worksheet retains a relationship with its data source that you can use to keep the query and data updated as well as use for other features. These tools are available from the External Data toolbar. Open **View**, point at **Toolbars**, and click **External Data**.

EDIT THE QUERY OR WIZARD

1. Select a cell in the external data range.

2. Click the first button on the left of the External Data toolbar. The button name changes depending on the type of external data you selected—for example, in text file ranges the button is named **Edit Text Import**; in data imported from the Web or Access databases, it's named **Edit Query**.

3. For data imported from:

  • A **text file** - In the Import Text File dialog box, verify the file name is correct, and click **Import**. Make any changes you want in the Text Import Wizard, clicking **Next** as necessary and clicking **Finish** when completed.

  • A **web page** - In the Edit Web Query dialog box, select or deselect tables on the displayed web page, or navigate to a new web site/page and make your selections there. Click **Import** when finished.

  • An **Access database** - In the Edit OLE DB Query dialog box, verify that the correct table name is displayed in the Command Text box. If not, change the name of the table in the Command Text box to the table you want. Click **OK**.

  • A **query you created** - In the Microsoft Query window shown in Figure 8-15, add/remove tables, criteria, and values. Open **File** and click **Return Data To Microsoft Office Excel** when finished. (A full description on how to use Microsoft Query is beyond the scope of the book. See *Microsoft Office Access 2003 QuickSteps*, published by McGraw-Hill/Osborne, for information on how to use these database features.)

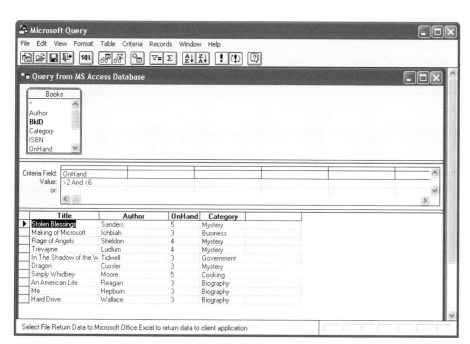

Figure 8-15: Microsoft Query is an add-in program that uses features that are more familiar to users of Access

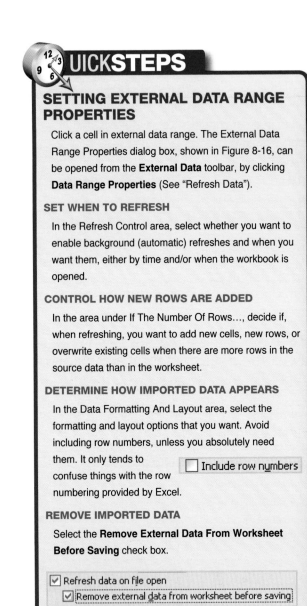

QUICKSTEPS

SETTING EXTERNAL DATA RANGE PROPERTIES

Click a cell in external data range. The External Data Range Properties dialog box, shown in Figure 8-16, can be opened from the **External Data** toolbar, by clicking **Data Range Properties** (See "Refresh Data").

SET WHEN TO REFRESH

In the Refresh Control area, select whether you want to enable background (automatic) refreshes and when you want them, either by time and/or when the workbook is opened.

CONTROL HOW NEW ROWS ARE ADDED

In the area under If The Number Of Rows..., decide if, when refreshing, you want to add new cells, new rows, or overwrite existing cells when there are more rows in the source data than in the worksheet.

DETERMINE HOW IMPORTED DATA APPEARS

In the Data Formatting And Layout area, select the formatting and layout options that you want. Avoid including row numbers, unless you absolutely need them. It only tends to confuse things with the row numbering provided by Excel.

☐ Include row numbers

REMOVE IMPORTED DATA

Select the **Remove External Data From Worksheet Before Saving** check box.

☑ Refresh data on file open
☑ Remove external data from worksheet before saving

REFRESH DATA

External data can be updated, or *refreshed*, to transfer any changes in the source data to the data you imported in Excel.

1. Select a cell in the external data you want to update.

2. On the External Data toolbar, click:

- **Refresh Data**, to connect to the source data and update the data in Excel

- **Cancel Refresh**, to interrupt the updating of your original data with the changes in the source data

- **Refresh All**, to update all external data ranges in the workbook (it doesn't matter which cells are selected)

- **Refresh Status**, to display the External Data Refresh Status dialog box and view the status of in-progress refreshes

3. See the "Setting External Data Range Properties" QuickSteps for more options on refreshing data and other importing features.

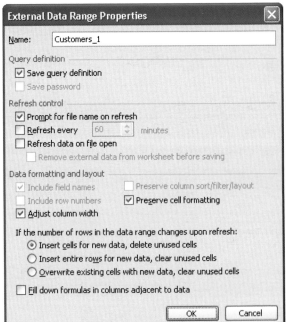

Figure 8-16: Control refresh and formatting options for imported data in the External Data Range Properties dialog box

How to...

- *Use Goal Seek*
- *Compare Alternatives Using Scenarios*
- *Use Multiple Variables to Provide a Result*
- *Save Solver Results and Settings*
- *Changing Solver Settings*
- *Create a PivotTable*
- *Create the PivotTable Layout*
- *Using PivotTables*
- *Create a PivotTable Chart*
- *Guard Workbooks with Passwords*
- *Using Passwords in a Shared Workbook*
- *Share a Workbook*
- *Merge Shared Workbooks*
- *Working with Changes in a Shared Workbook*
- *Protect a Shared Workbook*
- *Work with Views*
- *Protect Non-Shared Workbooks and Worksheets*

Chapter 9
Analyzing and Sharing Data

In this chapter you will learn how to use more advanced tools for manipulating your data to arrive at predetermined results that you want to achieve, how to reorient your data to give you different perspectives on how it is presented and interpreted, and how to protect your data when it is shared with others.

Get the Results You Want

Excel provides three features to help you find out how to arrive at a result by changing the underlying data. *Goal Seek* fills this requirement on a limited and temporary basis. *Scenarios* provides means to save and compare different sets of values that you can run to see how they affect your result. The most powerful feature in this suite of what-if analysis tools is *Solver*, an add-in program that extends the capabilities of Goal Seek and Scenarios.

Use Goal Seek

With Goal Seek, you choose a cell whose results are derived from a formula that uses the values in other cells. By seeing the change required in the value in one of the referenced cells, you see what it would take to achieve the result. To provide the answer you are looking for, Goal Seek requires three inputs:

- **Set Cell** is the cell address for the result you want. The Set Cell must contain a formula.

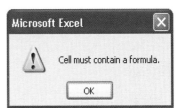

- **To Value** is the value (the goal) you want the formula in the Set Cell to achieve.

- **By Changing Cell** is the cell address for the value that you want to change in order to achieve the To Value (goal) you want. This cell must contain a value, not a formula, and must be referenced in the To Value's formula.

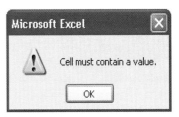

1. On a worksheet, enter a formula in a cell that will be your Set Cell.

2. Enter values needed in the formula in cells, one of which you'll chose to be the By Changing Cell.

3. Open **Tools** and click **Goal Seek**. The Goal Seek dialog box opens.

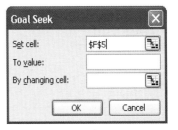

4. Select the cell that will be the Set Cell. The cell will be surrounded by a blinking border. If it is not correct, click a new cell.

5. In the To Value text box, type the new value you want the Set Cell to be.

6. Click the **By Changing Cell** text box, and then click the precedent cell on the worksheet that will need to change to accomplish your new Set Cell value. The cell will be surrounded by a blinking border, as shown in Figure 9-1.

7. Click **OK**. The cells will change value, and the Goal Seek Status dialog box opens and shows that a solution was found. Either:

- Click **OK** to accept the changes to your worksheet.

  –Or–

- Click **Cancel** to return the worksheet to its original values.

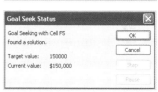

TIP

If you click **OK** in the Goal Seek Status and change the values on your worksheet, you can revert to the original values by using Undo.

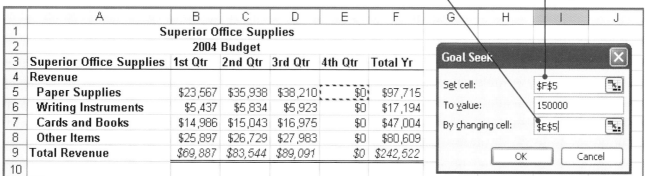

Changed cell will display what Paper Supplies' 4th quarter revenue must be to meet the goal

Set Cell is the amount of the total year goal entered in the To Value text box

Figure 9-1: Find what 4th quarter numbers must be to accomplish a total year goal

Compare Alternatives Using Scenarios

You use Scenarios to create a set of situations where you can change the values for various cells, save the changed values, and evaluate how the scenarios compare against one another in a side-by-side summary report. For example, if you wanted to see how changes to upcoming fourth-quarter revenue and expenses might affect your year-end profit, you could create a scenario for each entry on the worksheet that you want to change.

IDENTIFY CHANGING CELLS

1. Name the cells whose values you will be changing by clicking a cell and typing a name in the **Name** box at the left end of the Formula bar. Press **ENTER**. (It will be more meaningful to see descriptive names in the Scenario Values dialog box.)

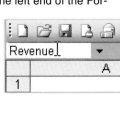

Named cells are often more readily understood...

...than cell addresses

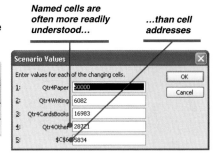

2. Repeat for the other cells that you will be changing.

CREATE A SCENARIO

1. Open **Tools** and click **Scenarios**. In the Scenario Manager, click **Add**. The Add Scenario dialog box opens.

2. In the Scenario Name text box, name the scenario according to the type of changes it contains—for example, Revenue, Low Wages, or Current Values.

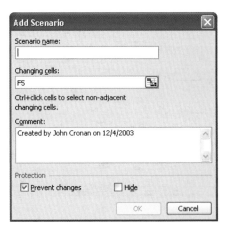

3. Click the **Changing Cells** text box, and then click the first cell where you will change a value. Press and hold **CTRL** while clicking any other cells whose values you'll want changed in this scenario. Move the dialog box or click the **Collapse Dialog** button if the dialog box is in your way. Expand the dialog box by either clicking **Close** or by clicking the **Expand Dialog** button.

4. In the Comment text box, edit the text by selecting the default text and entering your own.

5. Leave the **Prevent Changes** check box selected, unless you want the changes to replace the current values on the worksheet.

6. Click **OK**. If one of your selected cells contains a formula, you will be told that formulas in those cells will be replaced by constant values when you show the scenario. Click **OK** to continue.

Microsoft Excel

⚠ At least one of the changing cells you specified contains a formula. Formulas in changing cells will be replaced by constant values when you show a scenario.

OK

7. Either:

• Click **Add** to continue adding more scenarios.

–Or–

• In the Scenario Values dialog box, change the values for one or more of the listed changing cells, and click **OK**.

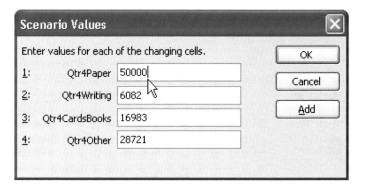

RUN A SCENARIO

1. Open the **Scenario Manager**, if necessary. Select the scenario you want to run and click **Show**, or double-click the scenario. The changing cells on your worksheet display any changed values, and any affected formulas recalculate and provide updated results.

2. To return your worksheet to its original state, click **Close**, and then click **Undo** on the Standard toolbar.

EDIT A SCENARIO

1. Open the **Scenario Manager**, if necessary, and select the scenario you want to edit. Click **Edit**.

2. In the Edit Scenario dialog box, change the name, add or remove changing cells, edit comments, and choose whether to change the protection status. Click **OK**.

3. In Scenario Values dialog box, make any changes to the values for the changing cells. Click **OK**.

4. To delete the scenario, select it and click **Delete**.

COMPARE SCENARIOS

1. Open the **Scenario Manager**, if necessary, and click the **Summary** button.

2. In Scenario Summary dialog box, leave the default option, **Scenario Summary**, selected.

3. Click the **Result Cells** box and then click the first cell where you want to see the result of the change(s) you made in scenarios.

4. If there is more than one results cell you want to see, type a comma (,) after the previous results cell before you click the subsequent cell.

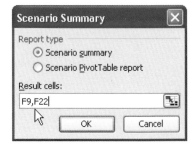

5. Click **OK** when finished. A new worksheet named Scenario Summary is added to the workbook, similar to Figure 9-2.

Figure 9-2: The Scenario Summary lists changing cells from all scenarios and shows how each scenario changes the results cells you have chosen

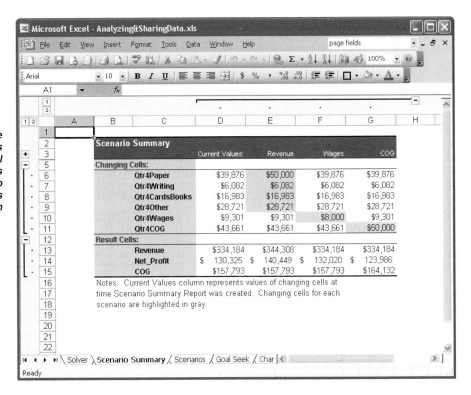

Use Multiple Variables to Provide a Result

Solver is Excel's most sophisticated tool for providing an answer to what-if problems. Figure 9-3 shows an example worksheet where Solver could be used. Solver is used by identifying the following cells and parameters:

- **Target cell** is the cell that contains a formula that you want to maximize, to minimize, or to return a specific value.

- **Changing (adjustable) cells** are related, directly or indirectly, to the target cell-by-cell references, and Solver will adjust them to obtain the result you want in the target cell.

- **Constraints** are limitations or boundaries you set for cells that are related, directly or indirectly, to the target cell.

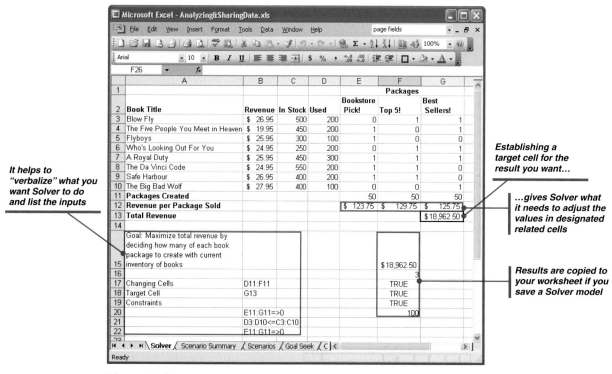

Figure 9-3: Solver provides a solution to a problem having multiple variables and constraints

TIP

If you run into problems opening Solver after you've installed it, open **Tools** and click **Add-Ins**. In the list of available **Add-ins**, verify that **Solver Add-in** has a check mark in its check box. If not, click the check box and click **OK**.

INSTALL SOLVER

1. Open **Tools** and click **Add-Ins**.

2. In the Add-Ins dialog box, select **Solver Add-in** and click **OK**.

3. You might see a message box informing you that Solver is not currently installed and giving you the opportunity to install it. Click **Yes**. You also might need your Office CD or path to a network installation location to complete the installation.

4. After the installation is completed, a new option, *Solver*, is added to the Tools menu.

SET UP SOLVER

1. Open **Tools** and click **Solver**. The Solver Parameters dialog box opens, as shown in Figure 9-4.

2. Click the **Set Target Cell** text box, and either type the address of the cell in which you want to see the result or click that cell on the worksheet. (If the dialog box is in your way, click the **Collapse Dialog** button and then click the cell. Click the **Expand Dialog** button to return to the full-size Solver Parameters dialog box.)

3. In the Equal To area, select what type of value you want the target cell to return: maximized, minimized, or a value you enter.

4. Click the **By Changing Cells** text box. Type the address of the first cell whose value you want Solver to adjust, or click that cell on the worksheet. Press and hold **CTRL** while clicking any other cells whose values you want Solver to adjust.

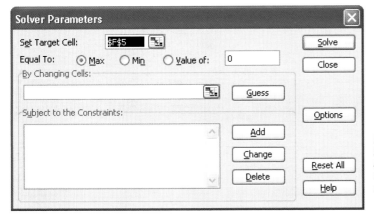

Figure 9-4: Setting the target cell, indicating what cells are to be changed, and listing constraints in the Solver Parameters dialog box provides all that's needed to run Solver

5. If you have constraints, click **Add** to open the Add Constraint dialog box.

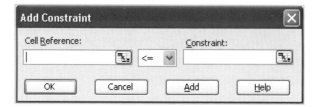

6. Click the **Cell Reference** text box. Type the cell reference that will be subject to your constraint, or select that cell reference on the worksheet.

7. Open the drop-down list of comparison operators and select the one that matches your constraint. Choosing **int** (whole numbers) or **bin** (1 or 0) places *integer* or *binary* in the Constraint text box.

8. Click **Add** to create another constraint, or click **OK** to finish adding constraints. The constraints are displayed in the Subject To The Constraints list box.

9. Click **Solve**. The Solver Results dialog box lets you know (or not) that a solution was reached.

Save Solver Results and Settings

You can save the work you do in Solver in several ways.

SAVE VALUES

After running a Solver problem, in the Solver Results dialog box, click **Keep Solver Solution**. The values produced by Solver are added to the worksheet, replacing your original numbers. Save the worksheet by pressing CTRL+S.

TIP

If you're not sure which cells to select for changing cells, clicking **Guess** will have Solver return all nonformula cells referenced by the formula in the target cell.

SAVE AS A SCENARIO

You can save different sets of changing cells values as scenarios whose results you can compare (see "Compare Scenarios" earlier in the chapter).

1. In the Solver Results dialog box, click **Save Scenario**. The Save Scenario dialog box opens.

2. Type a descriptive name for the scenario, and click **OK**.

3. Open **Tools** and click **Scenarios** to view and work with saved Solver and other scenarios.

SAVE SOLVER SETTINGS AS A MODEL

You can save the settings you've created in Solver as a *model*. These settings are copied onto the worksheet as well as are made available for you to run at a later time. You can have more than one Solver model saved per worksheet.

1. In the Solver Parameters dialog box, enter your settings and click **Options**. In the Solver Options dialog box, click **Save Model**.

2. In the Save Model dialog box, accept or change the range on the worksheet to where the Solver settings will be copied. Each constraint evaluation and three other cells containing parameters of the model are displayed, as shown in Figure 9-5.

3. Click **OK**.

NOTE

To add the settings of a previously saved model in Solver, open Tools, select **Solver**, and click **Options**. In the Solver Options dialog box, click **Load Model**. Select the range that contains the model settings you want to use, and click **OK** in any dialog boxes that might pop up until you return to the Solver Parameters dialog box.

Figure 9-5: Solver models save problem-solving settings directly on the worksheet

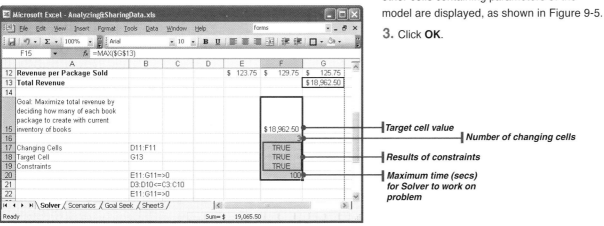

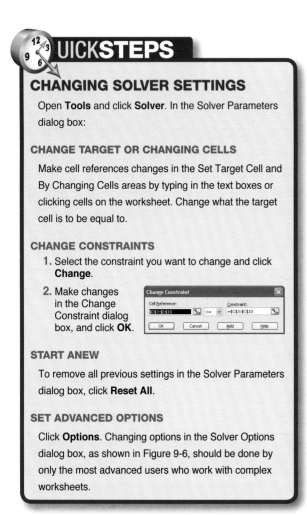

QUICKSTEPS

CHANGING SOLVER SETTINGS

Open **Tools** and click **Solver**. In the Solver Parameters dialog box:

CHANGE TARGET OR CHANGING CELLS

Make cell references changes in the Set Target Cell and By Changing Cells areas by typing in the text boxes or clicking cells on the worksheet. Change what the target cell is to be equal to.

CHANGE CONSTRAINTS

1. Select the constraint you want to change and click **Change**.
2. Make changes in the Change Constraint dialog box, and click **OK**.

START ANEW

To remove all previous settings in the Solver Parameters dialog box, click **Reset All**.

SET ADVANCED OPTIONS

Click **Options**. Changing options in the Solver Options dialog box, as shown in Figure 9-6, should be done by only the most advanced users who work with complex worksheets.

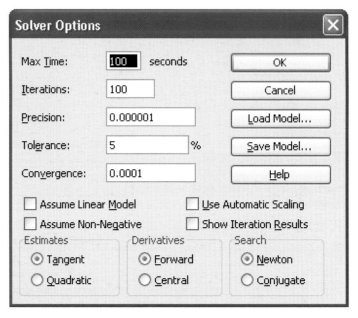

Figure 9-6: The Solver Options dialog box provides settings that typical users will seldom need to change

TIP

If you feel you need to give Solver more time or more attempts at reaching a solution, increase the **Max Time** and **Iterations** settings in the Solver Options dialog box. The maximum for each is 32,767 (seconds or interim calculations).

Work with PivotTables

PivotTables are Excel's "Swiss Army Knife" solution for comparing and analyzing data, especially in larger worksheets. A wizard helps you create the initial PivotTable report and lets you quickly make changes that pivot the table, rearranging the data for different solutions. Additionally, the PivotTable and PivotChart Wizards are used to create charts that graphically show the results of a PivotTable report.

Create a PivotTable

TIP

To return to the PivotTable And PivotChart wizard after a PivotTable is created, open **PivotTable** on the PivotTable toolbar, and click **PivotTable Wizard**.

NOTE

As shown in Figure 9-7, you can use a PivotTable to analyze external data. If you are unfamiliar with importing external data, see Chapter 8. You can also consolidate data from multiple ranges. Select the appropriate option, and follow the additional steps in the wizard.

1. Select a cell in a list whose data you want to use in the PivotTable.

2. Open **Data** and click **PivotTable And PivotChart Report**. The PivotTable And PivotChart Wizard dialog box opens to the first step in the process of creating a PivotTable, as shown in Figure 9-7.

3. Either:

   - Click **Finish** to create the PivotTable using the entire list and placing the blank PivotTable report on a separate worksheet, as shown in Figure 9-8.

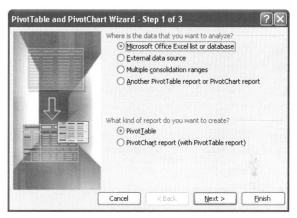

Figure 9-7: Creating a PivotTable for most lists is usually a one-step process

   –Or–

   - Click **Next** to continue the wizard to select the range whose data you want to use in the PivotTable and/or to choose where you want it located.

Layout area

Column headings

PivotTable toolbar

Drop Data Items Here

Figure 9-8: The initial PivotTable report displays a blank layout area and a PivotTable Field List that is derived from the column headings in the list

NOTE

PivotTables can be a bit overwhelming at first use. Keep trying to apply them; they can be very powerful.

Create the PivotTable Layout

1. Use the PivotTable And PivotChart Wizard to create a blank layout area, similar to Figure 9-8.

2. Drag an item from the PivotTable Field list to one of the boxes listed below, according to what you want to do.

- **Drop Row Fields Here** box allows you to display each category of that item in its own row. Typically, these items are descriptive and identifying, not numerical—for example, Country, Salesperson, and Title.

- **Drop Column Fields Here** box allows you to display each category of the item in its own column. Typically, these items are descriptive and identifying, not numerical—for example, Population, Sales, and Pages.

- **Drop Data Items Here** box allows you to sum or otherwise perform calculations and display the results. Typically, these items are numerical and capable of being counted, summed, and calculated.

3. Repeat Step 2 to create the layout that displays the information you want. You can drop more than one item in a box, and you can drag an item from a box on to the worksheet (outside the layout area) to remove it. See Figure 9-9 for an example of using multiple PivotTable Field list items in a row field arrangement.

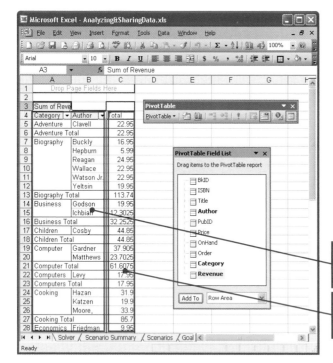

Drag multiple items to the Drop Row Fields Here box, and place them in the order you want for subtotals and totals

The Drop Data Item shows as a sum in this case

Figure 9-9: You can create totals and subtotals by dragging multiple PivotTable Field list items to the Row Fields box

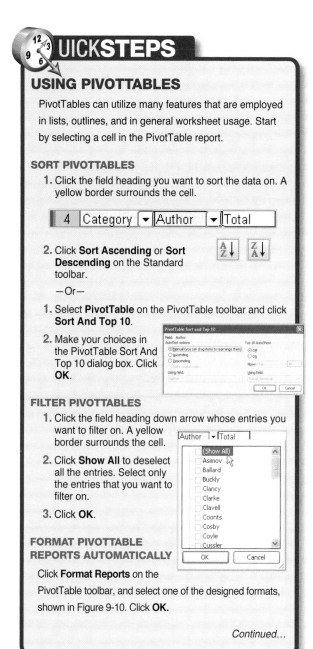

QUICKSTEPS

USING PIVOTTABLES

PivotTables can utilize many features that are employed in lists, outlines, and in general worksheet usage. Start by selecting a cell in the PivotTable report.

SORT PIVOTTABLES

1. Click the field heading you want to sort the data on. A yellow border surrounds the cell.

2. Click **Sort Ascending** or **Sort Descending** on the Standard toolbar.

   —Or—

1. Select **PivotTable** on the PivotTable toolbar and click **Sort And Top 10**.

2. Make your choices in the PivotTable Sort And Top 10 dialog box. Click **OK**.

FILTER PIVOTTABLES

1. Click the field heading down arrow whose entries you want to filter on. A yellow border surrounds the cell.

2. Click **Show All** to deselect all the entries. Select only the entries that you want to filter on.

3. Click **OK**.

FORMAT PIVOTTABLE REPORTS AUTOMATICALLY

Click **Format Reports** on the PivotTable toolbar, and select one of the designed formats, shown in Figure 9-10. Click **OK**.

Continued…

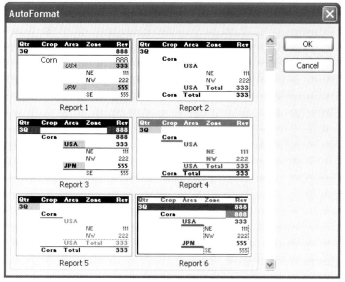

Figure 9-10: Quickly jazz up a PivotTable report by choosing a designed format

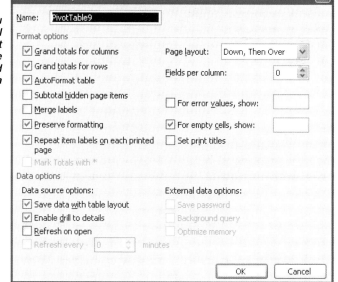

Figure 9-11: You can set several options that affect PivotTable formatting and data

USING PIVOTTABLES (Continued)

USE OUTLINING

Select the rows or columns you want to affect (see Chapter 8 for more information on grouping and outlining).

- Click **Hide Detail** or **Show Detail** on the PivotTable toolbar to collapse or expand the selected rows and columns

- Open **PivotTable** on the PivotTable toolbar, and point at **Group And Show Detail**. Click **Group** to add an outlining bar next to the selected rows or columns, enabling you to collapse and expand them by clicking the boxes at the ends of the outlining bar. Click **Ungroup** to remove the outlining bar.

6	Adventure Total		22.95
7	Biography	Buckly	16.95
8		Hepburn	5.99
9		Reagan	24.95
10		Wallace	22.95
11		Watson Jr.	22.95
12		Yeltsin	19.95
13	Biography Total		113.74
14	Business	Godson	19.95

SET FORMATTING AND DATA OPTIONS

Select a cell in the PivotTable report, open **PivotTable** on the PivotTable toolbar, and click **Table Options**. In the PivotTable Options dialog box, shown in Figure 9-11, choose the options you want, and click **OK**.

Create a PivotTable Chart

1. Select a cell in the PivotTable report, open **PivotTable** on the PivotTable toolbar, and click **PivotChart**. A new chartsheet is created with PivotTable layout boxes and field buttons surrounding the center data/plot area.

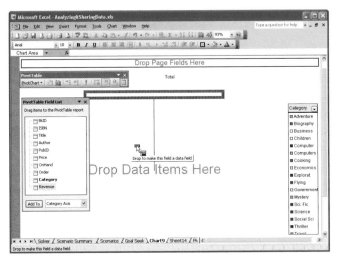

Figure 9-12: Similar to creating PivotTables, you lay out the PivotChart by dragging field list buttons to where they are applied

2. If necessary, drag items from the PivotTable Field list to the applicable field boxes on the PivotChart layout, as shown in Figure 9-12, to build the chart (see Chapter 6 for information on building a chart).

   - Right-click a chart item to see a menu of options that apply to that selected item. For example, you can right-click the displayed chart, select **Chart Type**, and select a different chart.

   - Double-click a chart item to open a formatting dialog box that applies to the selected item.

3. Click **Print Preview** on the Standard toolbar to see a clean view of the chart, similar to Fig 9-13. Click **Close** to return to the PivotChart.

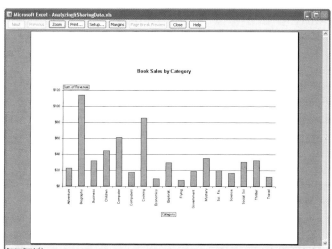

Figure 9-13: Using the chart techniques covered in Chapter 6, you can format a PivotChart to look the way you want

Work with Others

There are several ways to let others work with your data. One way is to control total access to the workbook file, choosing whether to allow others to open the file and/or make modifications. Another way is to provide access to the workbook and *protect* certain elements of the workbook and individual worksheets. You can also *share* the workbook so all can edit the same data, even simultaneously, while exercising limited protection.

Guard Workbooks with Passwords

The first level of security Excel offers is very simple. If you know the correct password, you can open and/or modify the file.

1. With an Excel wordbook open, open **File** and click **Save As**.

2. In the Save As dialog box, select **Tools** on the toolbar, and click **General Options**. In the Save Options dialog box, File Sharing area:

   - Type a password in the **Password To Open** text box to control who can open the workbook.

   - Type a password in the **Password To Modify** text box to control who can modify contents. (Leaving this password blank allows everyone to make changes; adding a password effectively provides read-only access to those who do not have the password.)

   - Select **Read-only Recommended** to prevent changes without requiring a password.

3. Click **OK**. Type the password a second time, and click **OK**.

4. Click **Save**. If you are working with an existing workbook, click **Yes** to replace the current file.

Share a Workbook

Shared workbooks are particularly useful for users on a network when multiple people are adding and viewing data in lists (see Chapter 8 for more information on creating and using lists). However, Excel does impose several limitations on what can be accomplished in a shared workbook. Before the workbook is shared by you or by the originating user, much of the "design work" of a worksheet should be completed. Shared workbooks are best used for entering and editing data, not making major structural changes. Many of the features that cannot be changed after a worksheet is shared are:

Charts	Merged cells
Conditional formats	Outlines
Data tables	PivotTable reports
Data validation	Scenarios
Graphics (including pictures, OLE objects, and drawing shapes)	Subtotals
Hyperlinks	Workbook protection
Macros	Worksheet protection

1. Open **Tools** and click **Share Workbook**.

2. In the Share Workbook dialog box, shown in Figure 9-14, select the **Allow Changes By More Than One User At The Same Time** check box. Click **OK**.

3. Click **OK** in the confirmation dialog box to continue. The workbook is shared and is so indicated by the word *Shared* added next to the workbook name in the Excel window title bar.

Do not forget or lose the password! When you password protect the opening of the file, the workbook is encrypted. There is virtually no way to open the workbook without the password. Unless this level of protection is absolutely needed, it might be better to use control features that are more selective and are described later in this section.

Sharing a *workspace* is not the same as sharing a workbook. Shared workspaces are areas on Microsoft Windows SharePoint Services web sites where people can access documents and other data. You can create a workspace and copy a workbook to it from the Shared Workspace task pane.

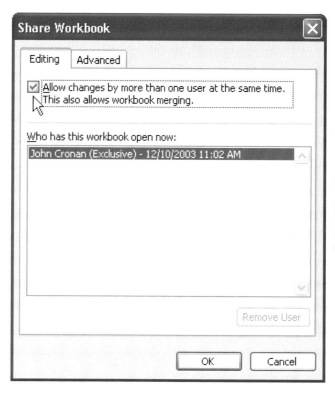

Figure 9-14: The Share Workbook dialog box lets you designate sharing of your workbook and shows who has a copy of it open

If you want to password-protect a shared workbook from the possibility of someone removing the tracked changes history, create the password before you share the workbook. To do this, see "Protect a Shared Workbook" rather than use the information in this section of this book.

Merge Shared Workbooks

Copies of the same shared workbook can be worked on by several users *offline* (not logged on to the network), and the changes can be merged into one document.

1. Move all copies of the workbook to be merged into one folder. You might have to rename one or more files, as you cannot have workbooks with the same name in the same folder.

2. Open the copy that will accept the merged data.

3. Open **Tools** and click **Compare And Merge Workbooks**. In the Select Files To Merge Into Current Workbook dialog box, select the first copy to be merged. Press and hold **CTRL** while clicking other workbooks you want to merge, shown in Figure 9-15.

4. Click **OK**.

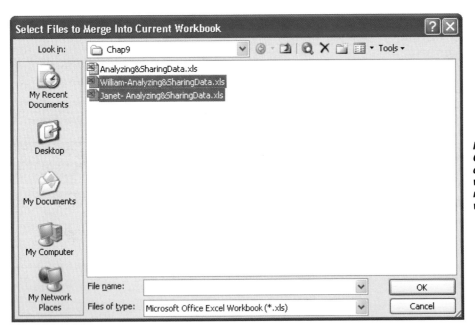

Figure 9-15: Changes in offline copies of a shared workbook can be merged into one workbook

WORKING WITH CHANGES IN A SHARED WORKBOOK

When sharing a workbook, you can adjust how often changes are kept, when they're updated, and how to resolve conflicts.

ENABLE TRACKING OF CHANGES (WORKBOOK NOT ALREADY SHARED)

When you enable Track Changes, you will also share the workbook.

1. Open **Tools**, point at **Track Changes**, and click **Highlight Changes**.

2. Select **Track Changes While Editing**. Click **OK** to close the Highlight Changes dialog box. Click **OK** again to save the now-shared workbook. (If the workbook has not yet been saved, you will be given the opportunity to name it.)

Highlight Changes

☑ Track changes while editing. This also shares your workbook.

MODIFY CHANGE ATTRIBUTES

1. Open **Tools**, point at **Track Changes**, and click **Highlight Changes**.

   - To highlight all changes, deselect the **When**, **Who**, and **Where** check boxes.

   - To selectively highlight changes, select options from the **When** and/or **Who** drop-down list boxes, and/or click the **Where** text box and select the range where you want changes highlighted.

   - To view changes onscreen, select **Highlight Changes On Screen**.

   - To view changes on a separate worksheet, select **List Changes On a New Sheet**. A History worksheet is added to the workbook, as shown in Figure 9-16.

Continued...

Protect a Shared Workbook

Shared workbooks are inherently not secure. (If you wanted them secure, you wouldn't share them.) However, you can protect against other users removing the shared workbook's change tracking feature and require that a password be used to unprotect it.

1. Open **Tools**, point at **Protection**, and click **Protect Shared Workbook**. (If you haven't already shared the workbook, you will see Protect And Share Workbook.)

2. In the Protect Shared Workbook dialog box, select **Sharing With Track Changes**.

3. Either:

   - Click **OK**. Click **OK** a second time to save the workbook.

   –Or–

   - Type a password and click **OK**. In the Confirm Password dialog box, type the password a second time and click **OK**. Click **OK** a third time to save the workbook. (If you are using a new workbook that hasn't yet been saved with a file name, you will be given that opportunity.)

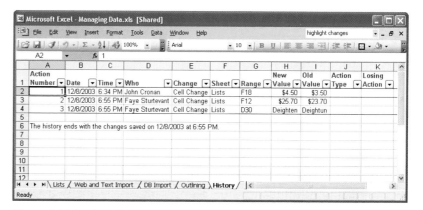

Figure 9-16: In shared workbooks, you can opt to have changes recorded on a separate History worksheet

WORKING WITH CHANGES IN A SHARED WORKBOOK *(Continued)*

2. Open **Tools**, point at **Share Workbook**, and click **Advanced**.

- To change whether and for how long changes are tracked, change the settings in the Track Changes area.

- To determine when changes are updated and whether to view changes by others, change the settings in the Update Changes area.

- To determine how conflicting changes are handled, in the Conflicting Changes Between Users area, determine how conflicts will be resolved.

ACCEPT OR REJECT CHANGES

1. Open **Tools**, point at **Track Changes**, and click **Accept Or Reject Changes**.

2. In the Accept Changes To Accept Or Reject dialog box, select options from the **When** and/or **Who** drop-down list boxes, and/or click the **Where** text box and select the range where you want changes highlighted. Click **OK**.

3. When a conflict arises from different users changing the same data, accept either your own or the change(s) made by the other user(s) in the Resolve Conflicts dialog box.

NOTE

Not all changes are tracked. Tracked changes include changes to cell contents created by editing, moving and copying, and inserting and removing rows and columns.

Work with Views

Although you can create custom views at any time, not just when working in a shared environment, the feature is especially useful when sharing a workbook. Each user's view can be saved with many personalized display settings, so the next time each user opens the workbook, the same worksheet that he or she was last working on will be displayed with the same print settings, filter settings, and other settings. Users can create other views and switch to them as well.

CREATE A CUSTOM VIEW

Set up any filters, print settings (including print areas), zoom magnifications, and other settings as you want them saved.

1. Open **View** and click **Custom Views**. The Custom Views dialog box lists your default *personal* view that appears when you open the workbook.

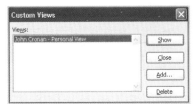

2. Click **Add**. In the Add View dialog box, type a descriptive name, choose whether to include print settings, filter settings, and hidden rows and columns. Click **OK**.

3. Set up and add any other views. Click **OK** when done.

Open **View** and click **Custom Views**. In the Custom Views dialog box, select the view you want to display, and click **Show**. To remove a view, select it and click **Delete**.

Protect Non-Shared Workbooks and Worksheets

If you generally "share" workbooks with others without formally creating a shared workbook, you can control whether several elements of both worksheets and workbooks can be changed.

PROTECT WORKSHEET ELEMENTS

Worksheet protection applies only to the currently active worksheet.

To protect all elements that can be protected:

1. Open **Tools**, point at **Protection**, and click **Protect Sheet**.

2. Ensure that the **Protect Worksheet And Contents Of Locked Cells** check box is selected. Optionally, type a password to unprotect the worksheet.

3. Deselect all check boxes in the **Allow All Users Of This Worksheet To** list box, and click **OK**. If necessary, confirm the password and click **OK**.

   –Or–

To protect elements selectively:

1. Select the range whose cells contain elements you want to selectively protect.

2. Open **Format**, point at **Cells**, and click **Protection**. Clear the **Locked** check box and click **OK**.

3. Open **Tools**, point at **Protection**, and click **Protect Sheet**.

4. Ensure the **Protect Worksheet And Contents Of Locked Cells** check box is selected. Optionally, type a password to unprotect the worksheet.

5. In the **Allow All Users Of This Worksheet To** list box, select the worksheet elements and actions you want the user to be able to perform. Click **OK**. If necessary, confirm the password and click **OK**.

PROTECT WORKBOOKS

1. Open **Tools**, point at **Protection**, and click **Protect Workbook**.

   - Select **Structure** to prevent changes to non-content aspects of the workbook, which include viewing hidden worksheets; inserting, moving, deleting, renaming, or hiding worksheets; moving and copying worksheets; and creating a scenario summary report.

   - Select **Windows** to prevent resizing and repositioning workbook windows.

2. Optionally, enter a password. Click **OK**. If necessary, confirm the password and click **OK**.

Chapter 10
Extending Excel

In the final chapter of this book, you will learn what lies beyond the mirror in Excel. You will see how to take Excel beyond the desktop to the Internet, how to create your own links, how XML (extensible markup language) can be used to make your data more useful, how to create macros to automate tasks, and how to use Excel by talking and listening.

Use Excel with Web Technology

The work you do in Excel is not confined to your computer. You can share workbooks, as described in Chapter 9, but you can extend well beyond that in breadth, as well as in capabilities, by making your work available to be displayed in Web browsers such as Internet Explorer. You can save or publish to web pages what you create in Excel—from entire workbooks to individual elements—such as worksheets, charts, ranges, and PivotTable reports. Excel converts your work to *HTML*, the *hypertext markup language* used to display text, graphics, and other items on the Internet and intranets. Additionally, you can choose to save or publish many elements to web pages with *interactive* capabilities, allowing users to not only view your work, but also to *use* your work to enter, change, sort, filter, and otherwise manipulate data.

Save or Publish a Workbook as a Web Page

The terms *save* and *publish* are often used together when speaking of creating Excel web pages, though they have quite different meanings. *Saving* a workbook as a web page is similar to saving a workbook with a different file name, that is, a copy is made of the original workbook in the folder you specify and that copy (with the extension .htm) replaces the original (with the extension .xls) that you see in the Excel window. Any new work you do is done in the open .htm file. Since you have the file open, it is not readily available for others to open (until you close it).

When you *publish* a workbook as a web page, you are sending an independent .htm copy to a folder, typically on a web server, for online use. Your original workbook file remains open in Excel (in .xls, .htm, or other formats), and the .htm copy you publish is available for others to open on the Web or on an intranet. Also, note that you can save an Excel file to several file formats, but you can only publish to .htm files.

1. Open the workbook you want to put on a web page.
2. Open **File** and click **Save As Web Page**. The familiar Save As dialog box opens with a few added options for saving or publishing web pages, as shown in Figure 10-1.
3. Browse to where you want the web page located. See the Tip on this page.

NOTE

Some of the features described in this chapter use advanced Excel tools and shared Office components that are not fully supported except by installation of Microsoft Office Professional Edition 2003.

NOTE

There are several benefits to saving or publishing your Excel work in in HTML. Perhaps the greatest benefit is that others do not need Excel to *view* your noninteractive worksheets. With just a connection to the Internet or with a local intranet and a computer (or similar device) with a browser (Internet Explore 4.01 or later), you can provide your data to anyone. However, for others to *use* the interactive features of Excel, users need to have Microsoft Internet Explorer 5.01 or later, and Microsoft Office 2003 Web Components (with license) installed on their machine. See www.microsoft.com to download these programs.

TIP

Click **My Network Places** in the Save As dialog box to find locations of web servers that can host your web page. To save (or publish) to a web server not shown in the list box, enter the web address of the server in the File Name box, in the form http://web address/path/file name. You will also need authorization from the owner of the web site or the web server administrator before you can add or modify files.

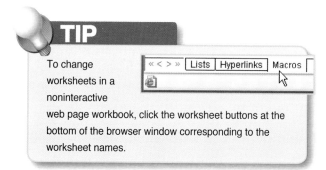

Figure 10-1:
The Save As dialog
box lets you select what
Excel data you want
saved to a web page
and choose whether to
add interactivity when a
web page file format is
selected

SAVE A NONINTERACTIVE WORKBOOK

You can only *save* an entire noninteractive workbook. If you try to *publish* an entire workbook, it will be published interactively.

1. In the Save area of the Save As dialog box, verify that **Entire Workbook** is selected.

2. Click **Change Title**. In the Set Page Title dialog box, type a descriptive title for the web page. This title appears in the title bar of the user's browser and helps to quickly identify the nature of the material on the page. Click **OK**.

3. Type the file name and click **Save**. Any features in your workbook not supported by Saving As A Web Page will be listed in a message box. Click **Yes** to continue. Figure 10-2 shows a noninteractive worksheet saved as a web page in Internet Explorer.

TIP

To change worksheets in a noninteractive web page workbook, click the worksheet buttons at the bottom of the browser window corresponding to the worksheet names.

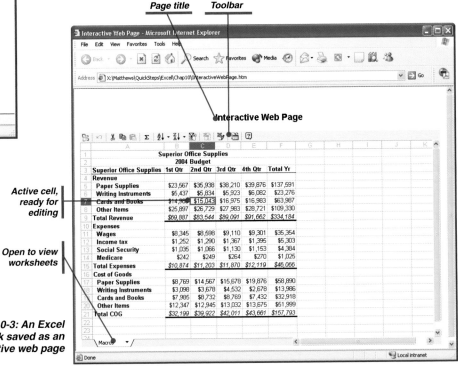

Worksheet tabs   **Page Title**   **Active worksheet's data initially displayed**

Figure 10-2: An Excel workbook saved as a noninteractive web page

SAVE AN INTERACTIVE WORKBOOK

1. In the Save area of the Save As dialog box, verify that **Entire Workbook** is selected, and select the **Add Interactivity** check box. (Notice that the Save As Type drop-down list box becomes unavailable, preventing you from saving it as anything other but .htm file format.)

2. Click **Change Title**. In the Set Page Title dialog box, type a descriptive title for the web page. This title appears in the title bar of the user's browser and helps to quickly identify the nature of the material on the page. Click **OK**.

3. Type the file name and click **Save**. Figure 10-3 shows an interactive worksheet saved as a web page in Internet Explorer.

Page title   **Toolbar**

Active cell, ready for editing

Open to view worksheets

Figure 10-3: An Excel workbook saved as an interactive web page

PUBLISH AN INTERACTIVE WORKBOOK

1. In the Save As dialog box, click **Publish**. In the Publish As Web Page dialog box, shown in Figure 10-4, open the **Choose** drop-down list in the Item To Publish area, and click **Entire Workbook**. Notice that the Add Interactivity With check box becomes unavailable, locking the check box in the selected state.

   ┌─────────────────┐
   │ Publish...   │
   └─────────────────┘

2. Click **Change** and type a descriptive title for the web page. This title appears in the title bar of the user's browser and helps to quickly identify the nature of the material on the page. Click **OK**.

3. Select one or both of the below, depending on what you want to do:

   - **AutoRepublish Every Time This Workbook Is Saved**, if you want to update the published .htm file whenever the workbook is saved

   - **Open Published Web Page In Browser**, if you want to open the page in your default web browser

4. Click **Publish**.

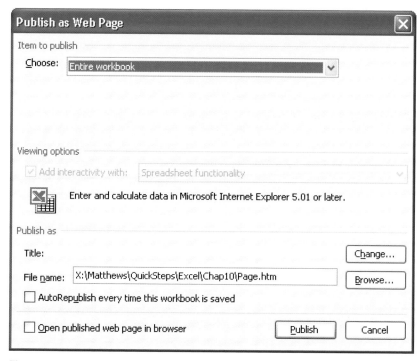

Figure 10-4: Choose which items of a workbook to publish and set options in the Publish As Web Page dialog box

Save Workbook Items as a Web Page

You can choose to save individual worksheets as well as choose to save selected objects and cells.

1. Open the workbook you want to put on a web page and select the item or range you want placed on the web page.

2. Open **File** and click **Save As Web Page**.

3. Browse to where you want the web page located.

4. In the Save area, click **Selection:*your selected element*.**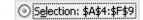

5. If you want to add interactivity, select **Add Interactivity**.

6. Click **Change Title,** and type a descriptive title for the web page. Click **OK**.

7. Type the file name and click **Save**.

TIP

To quickly view an opened Excel web page in your default browser, open **File** and click **Web Page Preview**.

CAUTION

Changing the name or location of web files should be done only by people experienced with HTML. Most web pages are interconnected, or *linked*, to other pages and objects, and changing their names or locations can cause problems when trying to open a page.

Publish Workbook Items

1. Open the workbook to be published.

2. Open **File** and click **Save As Web Page**.

3. Click **Publish**. In the Item To Publish area, open the **Choose** drop-down list box and select the item you want to publish.

4. If desired, select **Add Interactivity With** and choose the type of functionality you want.

5. Click **Change,** and type a descriptive title for the web page. Click **OK**.

6. Browse to where you want the web page published.

7. Select one or both of the below, depending on what you want to do:

   • **AutoRepublish Every Time This Workbook Is Saved** to update the published .htm file whenever the workbook is saved.

   • **Open Published Web Page In Browser** to open the page in your default web browser.

8. Click **Publish**.

CHOOSE A WORKSHEET

Click the worksheet tab at the bottom of the worksheet and select the worksheet you want from the text box of worksheet names.

SORT BY COLUMNS

Select a cell in the data you want to sort on.

* To sort in ascending order, select the **Sort Ascending** down arrow on the worksheet toolbar and click the column to sort on.

* To sort in descending order, select the **Sort Descending** down arrow on the worksheet toolbar and click the column to sort on.

FILTER DATA

1. Select a cell in the data you want to sort on.

2. Click the **AutoFilter** button on the worksheet toolbar. Down arrows are added to each column heading.

3. Click the **AutoFilter** down arrow in the column that you want to filter on and click the **Show All** check box to deselect all listed values in the column.

4. Click the value(s) whose records you want to view and click **OK**. Repeat for other columns as needed.

Continued…

Entire workbooks that are saved as web pages retain more changeable features than those web pages that are saved as items of a workbook. You may find that you have to open the source Excel workbook file (.xls), make your changes there, and then re-save as a web page.

Keep Web Pages Updated

You can make changes to web pages after you've saved them in .htm format and keep published pages up to date.

UPDATE NONINTERACTIVE WEB PAGES

1. In Excel, open the web page (.htm) that you want to change, and make any changes to content or formatting.

2. Open **File** and select **Save**, or click **Save** on the Standard toolbar.

3. Close the web page when finished.

UPDATE INTERACTIVE WEB PAGES

1. Open the source Excel workbook (.xls) from which you published the web page and make any changes to content or formatting. Click **Save**. (If you previously selected **AutoRepublish Every Time This Workbook Is Saved** in the Publish As Web Page dialog box, you're done! You may skip the next steps.)

2. Open **File**, select **Save As Web Page**, and click **Publish**.

3. In the Item To Publish area, open the **Choose** drop-down list box and select **Previously Published Items**. Select any items you don't want republished and click **Remove**.

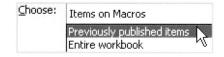

4. Click **Publish**.

5. Close the workbook when finished.

Package Excel Web Files

Excel data you save or publish for use in browsers is by default distributed across several files. To work under the provisions of HTML, the data is divided into several components and each is saved as a separate file. The main file is saved with an .htm file extension under the file name you specified. This web page pulls in data from the supporting files and displays the representation of what you see in Excel. The supporting files (and there can be quite a few!) are stored in a subfolder with the same name as the web page with *_files* added to

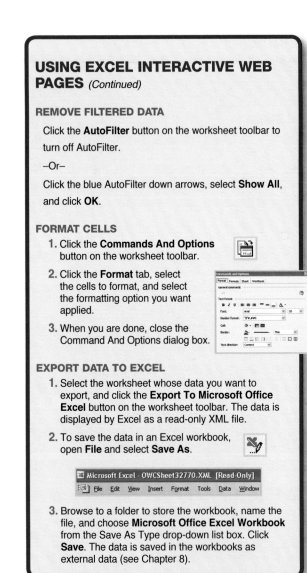

USING EXCEL INTERACTIVE WEB PAGES *(Continued)*

REMOVE FILTERED DATA

Click the **AutoFilter** button on the worksheet toolbar to turn off AutoFilter.

–Or–

Click the blue AutoFilter down arrows, select **Show All**, and click **OK**.

FORMAT CELLS

1. Click the **Commands And Options** button on the worksheet toolbar.

2. Click the **Format** tab, select the cells to format, and select the formatting option you want applied.

3. When you are done, close the Command And Options dialog box.

EXPORT DATA TO EXCEL

1. Select the worksheet whose data you want to export, and click the **Export To Microsoft Office Excel** button on the worksheet toolbar. The data is displayed by Excel as a read-only XML file.

2. To save the data in an Excel workbook, open **File** and select **Save As**.

3. Browse to a folder to store the workbook, name the file, and choose **Microsoft Office Excel Workbook** from the Save As Type drop-down list box. Click **Save**. The data is saved in the workbooks as external data (see Chapter 8).

the end of the name. You can choose, however, to have Excel save the web page and supporting files together, without benefit of a subfolder. You can also save the web page as a single file.

RENAME OR RELOCATE EXCEL WEB FILES

If you need to modify the name or the location of an Excel web page, you need to perform actions to both the web page and its subfolder.

1. Open **Start**, choose **My Computer**, and click **Folders** on the toolbar.

2. In the Folders pane to the left of the window, open the folder that contains the web page and subfolder.

3. In the right pane, perform the action you want.

- To **copy the web page**, select the .htm page, press and hold down CTRL while clicking the _files subfolder. Right-click either of the selected items, and click **Copy**. Open the destination folder in the left pane, right-click it, and click **Paste**.

- To **move the web page**, select the .htm page, press and hold down CTRL while clicking the _files subfolder. Right-click either of the selected items, and click **Cut**. Open the destination folder in the left pane, right-click it, and click **Paste**.

- To **rename the web page**, select the .htm page and press F2. Type the new name, making certain to add the .htm file extension. Select the _files subfolder and press F2. Type the same name as the web page, without the .htm, and add the _files at the end of the name.

CREATE WEB FILES IN THE SAME FOLDER

You can have Excel create the web page (main .htm file) placing all supporting files in the same folder instead of placing them in a subfolder.

1. In Excel, open **Tools**, choose **Options**, select the **General** tab, and click **Web Options**.

2. In the Web Options dialog box, click the **Files** tab and deselect the **Organize Supporting Files In A Folder** check box. Click **OK**.

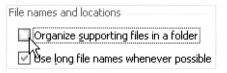

CREATE A SINGLE WEB PAGE

You can save the Excel elements you want onto a single file web page, or *.mhtm* file, in the same or another folder, avoiding the issues of dealing with a separate .htm file and supporting files. The downside to this is that its size will be larger and will take longer to load in the user's browser.

1. Open the workbook you want to put on a web page. If you want an element of the workbook on the single web page instead of the entire workbook, select it.

2. Open **File** and click **Save As Web Page**.

3. Browse to where you want the web page located.

4. In the Save area, choose either **Entire Workbook** or **Selection**.

5. In the Set Page Title dialog box, click **Change Title** and type a descriptive title for the web page. Click **OK**.

6. Open the **Save As Type** drop-down list box and select **Single File Web Page**.

7. Click **Add Interactivity** if you want to add it, and click **Save**.

Use Hyperlinks

Hyperlinks (or *links*) are items in documents that when clicked take you to other documents, different locations in the same document, other programs, and other locations. The Internet has brought links to mainstream use ("surfing the Web" is really just following a trail of several links), but hyperlinking is not just confined to web pages. For example, for each company in a worksheet you could create a hyperlink that would open Internet Explorer with that company's web site home page (see Figure 10-5). Additionally, you could create a link to a Word document that provides narrative support for a value in a balance sheet, or you could create a bookmark to take you to a specific cell.

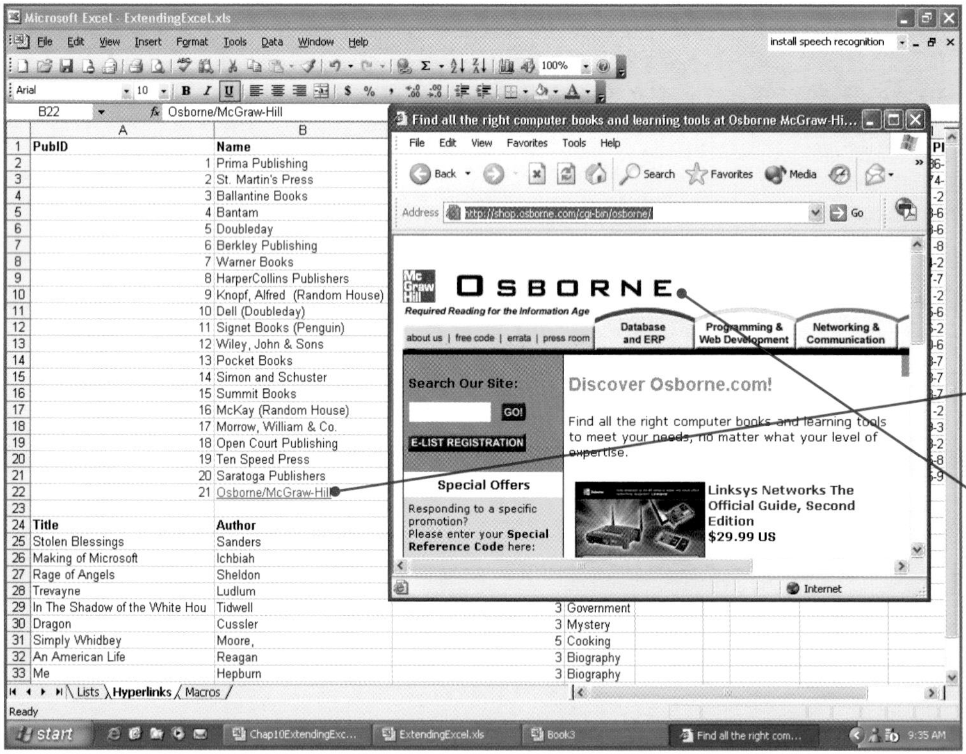

Figure 10-5: Creating a hyperlink in a worksheet connects your data with outside resources

CREATE A HYPERLINK

1. Select the cells, pictures, or other items you want to serve as the hyperlink.

2. Open **Insert** and select **Hyperlink**, or click **Insert Hyperlink** on the Standard toolbar.

3. In the Insert Hyperlink dialog box (shown in Figure 10-6) under Link To, select where the destination of the link will be.

   - **Existing File Or Web Page** opens a set of controls you can use to find a web address or file. Click the **Browse The Web** button to open your default browser to your home page. Click the **Browse To File** button to open a browse-type dialog box similar to the Open dialog box.

   - **Place In This Document** opens a text box where you can type a cell address and opens a list box where you can choose a cell reference or named reference.

   - **Create New Document** lets you name and locate a new Office document, and it opens the blank document in its parent program if you select **Edit The New Document Now**.

   - **E-mail Address** displays text boxes that you use to enter email address(es) and the subject of the message. When clicked, a new message dialog box opens in the default e-mail program with the address(es) displayed in the To box and the subject filled in, similar to Figure 10-7. (You can send to multiple addressees by using a semicolon (;) to separate each address.)

4. Click **OK**.

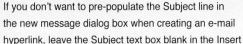

TIP

If you don't want to pre-populate the Subject line in the new message dialog box when creating an e-mail hyperlink, leave the Subject text box blank in the Insert Hyperlink dialog box.

E-mail address:

mailto:cbts@myisp.com;marty@hisisp.com

Subject:

Status of current chapter

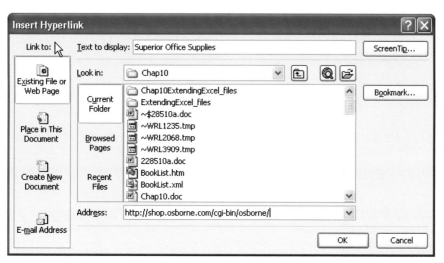

Figure 10-6: The Insert Hyperlink dialog box provides controls that allow you to tailor the destination of a clicked hyperlink

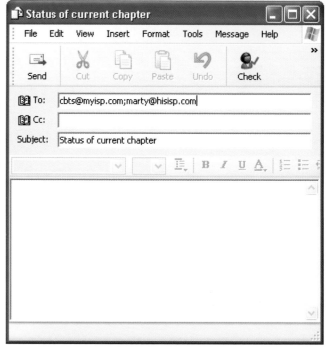

Figure 10-7: Creating an E-mail Address hyperlink opens a new message dialog box, pre-addressed and with the subject line filled in

CREATE A BOOKMARK

Bookmarks are locations within the current document that you can "jump" to.

1. Select the cells, pictures, or other items you want to serve as the hyperlink.

2. Open **Insert** and select **Hyperlink**, or click **Insert Hyperlink** on the Standard toolbar.

3. In the Insert Hyperlink dialog box, under Link To, select **Existing File Or Web Page**, and click **Bookmark** (on the far right of the dialog box).

4. In the Select Place In Document dialog box, shown in Figure 10-8, type a cell reference or select a named place that you want as the hyperlink destination (or bookmark).

5. Click **OK** twice.

Select Place in Document

Type in the cell reference:

B44

Or select a place in this document:

- Cell Reference
  - Lists
  - Hyperlinks
  - Macros
- Defined Names
  - Lists!DB1
  - Hyperlinks!Managing_Data
  - Hyperlinks!Query_from_MS_Access_Database

OK   Cancel

Figure 10-8: Use the Select Place In Document dialog box to designate where in the workbook the link will take you

EDIT A HYPERLINK

1. Click the cell or object that contains the hyperlink you want to change and hold down the mouse button until the pointer changes from the hyperlink pointer to a standard Excel pointer, or you might just need to press and hold the mouse button a few seconds. (Clicking a cell that contains a hyperlink will enact the hyperlink.)

2. Open **Insert** and select **Hyperlink**, or click **Insert Hyperlink** on the Standard toolbar. The Edit Hyperlink dialog box opens, similar to the Insert Hyperlink dialog box (see Figure 10-6).

3. Either:

   - Make changes to the hyperlink destination (see "Create a Hyperlink").

     –Or–

   - Click the **Remove Link** button to remove the hyperlink.

4. Click **OK**.

Plan for the Future

When you hear talk of the future of the Internet and how it will change our lives, you come across terms such as .NET (pronounced "dot net"), web services, and several others that are just now making their way into the general lexicon. The general premise of this next-generation change of our use of the Web is the sharing of information. Today, most data on the Internet is in a jumble of formats and structures that doesn't lend itself to being easily shared among web applications. Microsoft's solution to this (in very simplified terms) is to identify data using XML (extensible markup language), thus ensuring a common set of rules that govern how the data is organized—sort of a world-wide recognized database format. In this sense, once data is organized and formatted with XML *tags* (code that identifies the data, see Figure 10-9), every bit of data available on the Web can be easily retrieved by web applications to display meaningful results.

So what does all this have to do with Excel? Plenty. As you've seen throughout this book, Excel is all about data and how it's organized and managed. In this regard, XML and Excel are a natural team. In Excel, you can:

- Open XML files (.xml) and save the data as a workbook
- Attach XML *schemas* (files that create the data structure, similar to the fields used in databases and lists) to workbooks and *map* the XML elements to your existing data
- Use XML data from web services in your worksheets
- Use options from the XML subsidiary menu

Using XML in Excel is beyond the scope of this book, but if you want to get a head start on getting your data ready for the next evolution in computing and Internet use, give XML a deeper look.

NOTE

Several years ago Microsoft produced a video to demonstrate .NET that showed comedian Steve Masters as an accident-prone traveler. When lying on the street after being hit by a bicyclist, he was able to make one call on a web-enabled cell phone to his health provider. All the pieces of ensuing process—from patient identification, to patient history, to insurance limits, to appointment scheduling, to nearest clinic location, and so on—were quickly integrated and made available to Steve and his doctor by pulling in all this related data onto one screen.

Automate Excel

You can automate repetitive tasks in Excel by using *macros*. Macros are recorded either by keyboard and mouse actions or by using Microsoft Visual Basic for Applications (VBA), a programming language.

Use Recorded Macros

Repetitive tasks you perform in Excel can be *recorded* as a macro and re-run at later times. For example, if you formatted a worksheet differently for each of your division heads, you could record the formatting sequence for each. For next quarter's report, simply run each macro in turn to quickly get the tailored results you want. Though macros are small programs written in the Visual Basic for Applications (VBA) programming language, you don't have to know VBA or be a programmer to record and run macros.

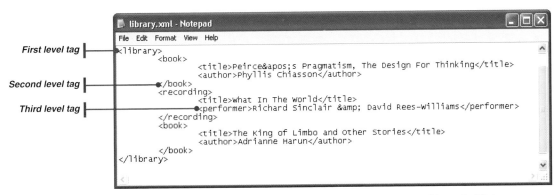

First level tag

Second level tag

Third level tag

Figure 10-9: XML tags (enclosed in angle brackets) can create a hierarchal list

NOTE

To record and run macros you might have to lower the security level of Excel a notch. Open **Tools**, point at **Macro**, and click **Security**. In the Security dialog box, shown in Figure 10-10, choose **Medium**, and click **OK**. Medium security is the lowest level needed to run macros while still providing a degree of protection by forcing you to choose whether to run each one. Macro security is important because macros are executable programs and can bring havoc to your system when used by hackers for malicious purposes.

RECORD A MACRO

1. Open **Tools**, point at **Macro**, and click **Record New Macro**.

2. In the **Macro Name** text box, create a name to identify the macro. Macro names must begin with a letter, and must not contain spaces or be the same name as a cell reference.

Figure 10-10: Medium security provides a compromise between not being able to run your own macros and leaving yourself vulnerable to unsafe macros

3. In the **Shortcut Key** text box (optional), type a letter (no numbers) to use in combination with CTRL that will run the macro. To use an uppercased letter, the key combination will be CTRL+SHIFT+*your letter*. (If you choose a shortcut key combination that Excel uses for other purposes, your shortcut will override Excel's when the workbook that contains the macro is open.)

4. In the **Store Macro In** drop-down list box, choose whether you want to store it in the current workbook, in a new workbook, or in your Personal Macro Workbook, which makes the macro available to workbooks other than the workbook in which it was created.

5. In the **Description** text box, type a description (optional) that helps you identify the nature of the macro.

6. Click **OK**.

7. Perform the steps involved to do the repetitive task. These steps might include opening dialog boxes, selecting settings, creating formulas, and applying formatting.

8. On the Macro toolbar:

   - Click **Relative References** (optional, see Chapter 2) to use relative cell references in the cell addresses.

   - Click **Stop Recording** to finish recording your actions as part of the macro and return to normal use.

TIP

If you record a step in the macro you don't want, you can open the macro in the Visual Basic Editor and remove the unwanted code. However, it is usually easier to delete the macro and start over.

DELETE A RECORDED MACRO

1. Open **Tools**, point at **Macro**, and click **Macros**.

2. In the Macro dialog box, shown in Figure 10-11, select the macro you want deleted and click **Delete**.

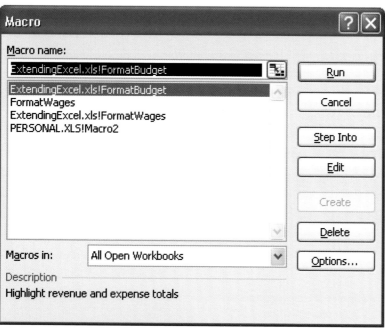

Figure 10-11: The Macro dialog box lists available macros and provides the tools to run, edit, set options, and remove them

ADD A MACRO TO A MENU OR TOOLBAR

If adding a toolbar button to a hidden toolbar, display the toolbar first.

1. Open the workbook that contains the macro you want to add unless the macro is stored in your Personal Macro Workbook.

2. Open **Tools** and click **Customize**. In the Customize dialog box, open the **Commands** tab.

3. Scroll the Categories list box, click **Macros**, and drag the **Custom Menu Item** to the location on the:

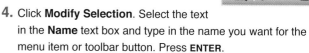

- **Toolbar**, where you want the button

  –Or–

- **Menu bar**, either on the menu bar itself or on an existing menu

4. Click **Modify Selection**. Select the text in the **Name** text box and type in the name you want for the menu item or toolbar button. Press **ENTER**.

Name:	Format Budget

5. Click **Modify Selection** a second time and select **Assign Macro**. In the Assign Macro dialog box, double-click the macro you want to assign to the menu item or button.

6. Click **Close**.

Edit a Macro

You can change minor attributes of a macro without using VBA. (To edit the code that defines the actions of the macro you will have use the Microsoft Visual Basic Editor, shown in Figure 10-12, whose discussion is beyond the scope of this book.)

1. Open **Tools**, point at **Macro**, and click **Macros**.

2. Select the macro you want to change and click **Options**.

3. In the Macro Options dialog box, change the shortcut key and/or the macro description.

4. Click **OK** when finished.

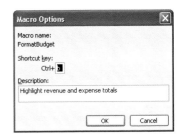

Macro name
Your description

Selected cells

Formatting instructions

Visual Basic code

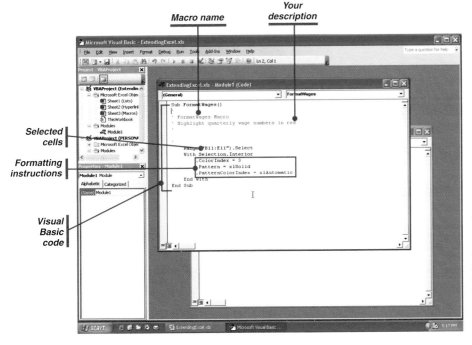

Figure 10-12: The Microsoft Visual Basic Editor provides a graphical palette for working on macros and other VBA code

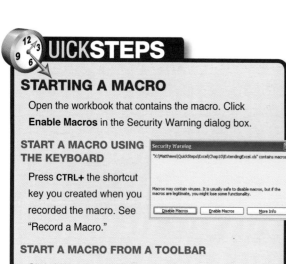

STARTING A MACRO

Open the workbook that contains the macro. Click **Enable Macros** in the Security Warning dialog box.

START A MACRO USING THE KEYBOARD

Press **CTRL+** the shortcut key you created when you recorded the macro. See "Record a Macro."

START A MACRO FROM A TOOLBAR

Click the toolbar button assigned to the macro. See "Add a Macro to a Menu or Toolbar."

START A MACRO FROM A MENU

See "Add a Macro to a Menu or Toolbar."

* Open the menu and click the menu item assigned to the macro.

  –Or–

* Click the menu name on the menu bar.

START A MACRO FROM A DIALOG BOX

1. Open **Tools**, point at **Macro**, and click **Macros**.
2. Select the macro and click **Run**, or double-click the macro.

NOTE

You will need supporting hardware to use the features described in the "Communicate with Excel" section, including a sound card, speakers, and a microphone. See *Windows XP QuickSteps*, published by McGraw-Hill/Osborne, for more information on setting up and using sound with your computer.

Communicate with Excel

Although we're still a ways away from being able to converse with our desktop computers in the manner of *2001: A Space Odyssey*'s HAL, we can start to get a glimpse of that world with the text-to-speech and speech recognition features available in Excel today.

Listen to Excel

1. Open **View**, point at **Toolbars**, and click **Text To Speech**, or right-click a toolbar and click **Text To Speech**. Click **Yes** if you are asked whether you want to install the feature. The toolbar displays on the worksheet.

2. Click the first cell that contains the text you want to be read. Either:

   * **Click By Rows**, to have the cells read across rows, top to bottom

   * **Click By Columns**, to have the cells read down columns, left to right

3. Select the cell where you want to start and click **Speak Cells**. The cell contents start being read back to you. To stop the voice readback, click **Stop Speaking**.

Tell Excel What to Do

You can use voice commands to perform basic navigation and editing duties. While not a replacement for the mouse and keyboard, speech recognition has its place in the overall computing experience.

ADD SPEECH RECOGNITION

1. Insert your Microsoft Office 2003 CD in its drive.
2. Click the Windows **Start** button and then click **Control Panel**.
3. In Windows Classic view, double-click **Add Or Remove Programs**.
4. Select Microsoft Office *your edition* 2003 and click **Change**.
5. In the Maintenance Mode Options dialog box, select **Add Or Remove Features** and click **Next**.

TIP

To have Excel read a particular cell's content when you press **ENTER** while in that cell, click **Speak On Enter** on the Text To Speech toolbar to turn that feature on. Select any cell and press **ENTER**. Click the button a second time to turn it off.

NOTE

The speech recognition feature in Office 2003 is geared predominately toward users of Microsoft Word. In fact, the easiest way to install it is to use the Tools menu Speech command in Word. I describe an alternative method in case you do not have Word available.

6. In the Custom Setup dialog box, select **Choose Advanced Customization Of Applications** and click **Next.**

7. In the Advanced Customization dialog box, click the plus (+) sign next to Office Shared Features, and then click the plus sign next to Alternative User Input. Click the **Speech** button and click **Run From My Computer**.

8. Click **Update**. When the update is complete, click **OK**, and close Add Or Remove Programs.

SET UP SPEECH RECOGNITION

1. If the Control Panel is not already open, click the Windows **Start** button and then click **Control Panel**.

2. In Windows Classic view, double-click **Speech**.

3. In the Speech Recognition tab, shown in Figure 10-13, step through the following wizards:

4. Click **Train Profile** to provide the speech recognition software an opportunity to "learn" your voice.

5. Click **Configure Microphone** to provide volume setting for the speech recognition software.

6. Click **OK** to close the Speech Properties dialog box.

Figure 10-13: The Speech Recognition tab provides the tools for you to "train" the software to your voice and adjust your microphone volume

DISPLAY THE LANGUAGE BAR

1. If the Control Panel is not already open, click the Windows **Start** button and then click **Control Panel**.

2. In Windows Classic view, double-click **Regional And Language Options**, select the **Languages** tab, and click **Details**.

3. In the Text Services And Input Languages dialog box, click the **Language Bar** button, and select **Show The Language Bar On The Desktop**.

   ☑ Show the Language bar on the desktop

4. Click **OK** three times to close the open dialog boxes, and click the **Close** button to close the Control Panel. The Language bar displays on your screen.

   🖉 Microphone 🔲 Dictation 🔻 Voice Command Starting Speech... 🔲 Tools 🔃 ⁝

USE SPEECH RECOGNITION IN EXCEL

1. On the Language bar, click **Microphone** to turn it on (if your microphone has a switch, ensure it is turned on as well). Text acknowledging your microphone is on appears next to the Microphone button.

2. Use voice commands in combination with the keyboard or mouse to accomplish tasks. For example, say "file" to open the File menu, or select a cell and say "bold."

   🖉 Microphone Bold

3. If your speech is not recognized, select **Tools** on the Language bar and click **Options**. Click **Train Profile** and read more passages to better train the software to your speech.

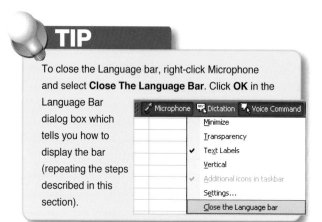

TIP

To close the Language bar, right-click Microphone and select **Close The Language Bar**. Click **OK** in the Language Bar dialog box which tells you how to display the bar (repeating the steps described in this section).

🖉 Microphone	🔲 Dictation	🔻 Voice Command
	Minimize	
	Transparency	
✓	Text Labels	
	Vertical	
✓	Additional icons in taskbar	
	Settings...	
	Close the Language bar	

filtering, 131, 141–142, 148–149
headings for, 15–17, 130, 165
hide/unhide, 36
in lists, 129–135
removing, 35
selecting, 26
sorting by, 131, 139–140
summary, 142
summing, 130, 134–135
comments, 26, 40–43, 74
communicating with Excel, 196–198
converting
decimals to fractions, 20
numbers to percentages, 21
numbers to scientific notation, 19, 21
text to data, 144–146
copying
charts, 90, 101
comments, 42
data into adjoining cells, 24
data onto other files, 27
formulas, 27–28, 57
Criteria button, 135
cropping, 121, 125
currency, 18, 20
curves, 116
customizing
headers and footers, 69
toolbars, 8–9

D

data
adding to charts, 102
analyzing, 103, 153–168
editing. *See* editing
entering. *See* entering
entry forms, 133–135
filtering, 130–131, 141–142, 148–149, 167, 183
finding, 28–29, 134–135
importing, 144–150
point. *See* values
range, 87–88, 152
replacing, 25, 28–30
selecting previously entered, 25
series, 84, 86–89, 93–99
sorting, 139–140, 167, 183
databases, 15, 130. *See also* Access
datasheet. *See* table

dates, 17–23, 70, 139
decimals, 18–20
deleting
comments, 41
data, 24–26
formulas, 58
macros, 194
worksheets, 50
See also removing
diagrams, 108, 119–120. *See* also graphics
docking, 7, 10, 92
doughnut charts. *See* pie charts
drawings, 107, 115. *See also* curves
Drawing toolbar, 102, 107–108, 115

E

editing
cell data, 24–25, 154–155
formulas, 56
imported data, 151–152
macros, 195
records, 132
scenarios, 158
entering
a logical series, 25
currency, 19–20
data with a form, 132–133
dates, 19–21
numbers, 18–19
text, 17–18
times, 22–23
error checking, 63–64, 136, 138
Excel
closing, 14
communicating with, 196–198
exporting web pages to, 184
personalizing, 7–9
starting, 1–2
external data, 150–152
External Data toolbar, 151–152
external references, 59–60

F

files. *See* workbooks
fill handle, 25

filtering
  data, 130–131, 141–142, 148–149, 183
  PivotTables, 167
finding
  a workbook, 6
  and correcting errors, 63–66
  and replacing, 28–30
  data, 28–29, 134–135
  using the Indexing Service, 6
floating, 7
fonts, 34, 36, 40–41, 70
footers. *See* headers and footers
formatting, 33–50
  applying, 21, 26–27, 34–35, 39, 44–47
  automatic, 46, 120, 133
  charts, 93, 98–99
  comments, 42–43
  conditional, 26, 47
  dates, 22
  graphics, 121–125
  headers and footers, 70–71
  imported data, 152
  interactive web pages, 184
  numbers, 20–21
  outlines, 143–144
  phone numbers, 21
  PivotTables, 167–169
  SSNs, 21
  text, 40–47
  times, 24
  ZIP codes, 21
forms. *See* data, entry forms
Formula Auditing toolbar, 63–66
Formula bar, 3, 17–18, 20, 24–25
formulas, 3, 51–60
  building, 54–56
  copying, 27–28, 57
  editing, 56
  external references in, 59–60
  evaluating, 66
  moving, 57
  multiple variables in. *See* Solver
  recalculating, 58
  See also functions
fractions, 20–21
freeform, 115–116
functions, 3, 51, 54, 60–63

G

Getting Started task pane, 7
Goal Seek, 154–155
gradients, 121, 123
graphics, 107–127
  creating mirrored images of, 127
  formatting and modifying, 121–125
  grouping, 126
  positioning, 126–127
  See also diagrams; drawings; objects; pictures
gridlines, 74, 95–96
grids. *See* spreadsheets
grouping data, 143–144

H

handles, 7, 24, 25, 78, 93, 101, 105, 122–124, 126
headers and footers
  customize, 68–69
  formatting, 70–71
  insert pictures in, 70
  margins for, 71–72
  page numbers in, 71
headings
  adding drop–down lists to column, 141
  as title pages, 73
  column and row, 15–16, 48, 130–131
  printing, 74
Help, 3, 10–11, 62, 77
hide/unhide
  axes, 95
  cells and formulas, 176
  Office Assistant, 11
  rows and columns, 36, 144
HTML, 178, 183
hyperlinks, 186–189

I

identifying information, 5
importing data, 144–150
installing
  Microsoft Query, 148–149
  Solver, 161
  speech recognition, 196–197

interactive web pages, 178
  exporting data from, 184
  filtering data on, 183, 184
  formatting cells on, 184
  publishing, 181
  sorting data on, 183
  updating, 183
intersections, 16, 54

K

keyboard shortcuts
  for task panes, 7
  to calculate, 58
  to copy and move, 14, 42, 57
  to display the task pane, 7
  to find a function, 63
  to find data, 29, 30
  to open the Open dialog box, 5
  to print, 75
  to save, 162
  to select all cells, 26
  to start a new workbook, 5
  to view formulas, 53
keywords, 5, 6, 114

L

labels. *See* headings
Language bar, 198
legends, 84, 93, 96–97, 103
links. *See* external references; hyperlinks
lists, 130–135
locating. *See* finding
locking rows and columns, 48

M

macros, 191
  adding to menus and toolbars, 194
  deleting, 194
  editing, 195
  recording, 192–193
  starting, 196
margins, 71–72, 77–78
merging cells, 43

microphones, 197
Microsoft Query, 147–149, 151
Microsoft Visual Basic Editor, 191, 195
modifying. *See* editing
moving
  data, 25–26
  files and folders, 13–14
  formulas, 57
  graphics, 126–127
  the task pane, 7
  toolbars, 10

N

naming
  cells, 54
  workbooks, 12–13
  worksheets, 50
.NET, 190
noninteractive web pages, 178
  saving, 179, 182
  updating, 183
numbers
  entering, 18–19
  formatting, 20–21

O

objects, 91, 104, 189
  adding from other programs, 115–117
  See also graphics
Office Assistant, 11
organizational charts, 119–120
Organization Chart toolbar, 119
organizing. *See* sorting
orientation
  of pages, 72, 74
  of text, 42–43
  of pictures, 70
  of WordArt, 119
outlining, 139, 142–144, 168

P

page breaks, 77, 79, 103
page numbers, 68, 70

Page Setup. *See* printing
passwords, 169–171,173, 175–176
Paste Special, 27–28
pasting. *See* copying; Paste Special
patterns, 39–40, 98, 121, 123
percentages, 20, 21
phone numbers, 21
photos. *See* pictures
pictures, 107–110
  adding to headers and footers, 70
  creating, 111
  cropping, 125
  inserting into charts, 101–102
  using as backgrounds, 124
  See also graphics
Picture toolbar, 121
pie charts, 86, 105
PivotTables, 164–169
PivotCharts, 168-169
preview print, 75–79, 104, 168
print areas, 74–76
printers, 80–81
printing, 11, 67–82
  comments, 74
  multiple copies, 82
  options, 74, 81
  order 74
  selections, 75–76
  to a file, 81
  See also headers and footers
Print Preview toolbar, 77, 103
protecting
  graphics, 127
  scenarios, 158
  workbooks, 169–171, 173, 175–176
publishing web pages, 178–179, 181, 182

R

ranges, 26–27
records. *See* rows
referencing cells, 51–54
refreshing data. *See* updating
removing
  cells, columns, rows, 34–35
  effects, 124
  hyperlinks, 189
  lists, 134
  passwords, 170

validation criteria, 137
  See also deleting
renaming
  Excel web files, 184
  named references, 157
  worksheets, 50
research on the Internet, 11
resizing
  charts, 101
  graphics, 122, 124–125
  text boxes, 102
Restore button, 133
rotating
  graphics, 123–125
  pie charts, 104
rows
  adding, 34–35, 131–132
  adjusting height of, 34–35
  as database records, 15–16, 130, 132
  headings for, 15–16, 48
  hide/unhide, 36
  numbered headers on, 15–17
  removing, 34–35
  selecting, 26
  sorting by, 140
  summary, 142–144
  Total, 130, 134–135

S

saving
  automatically, 12
  custom charts, 100
  graphics, 108
  Solver results and settings, 162–164
  templates, 14
  web pages, 179–180
  workbooks, 12–13
  See also publishing
scaling for print, 72–73, 98
scanner, selecting pictures from a, 110–111
scenarios, 153, 156–159, 163
scientific notation, 18, 21
selecting
  cells, rows, and columns, 26
  chart items, 93
  graphics, 109
sharing
  printers, 80

workbooks, 169–174
workspaces, 171
shortcuts
  creating to start Excel, 2
  for quickly adding data, 24–25
  to copy a comment, 42
  to create a new workbook, 4
  to frequently used programs, 3
  to Help, 10
  to the Open dialog box, 5
  to open a workbook, 5
show/hide. *See* hide/unhide
shrink text to fit, 43
Solver, 153, 160–164
sorting
  data, 139–140
  in PivotTables, 167
  in web pages, 183
  with queries, 147–146
special effects for text. *See* WordArt
speech recognition, 196–198
spelling, 30–31
spinner, 19
splitting
  cells, 38
  worksheets, 49
spreadsheets, 3, 16
SSNs, 21
styles. *See* formatting
summing, 63

T

tables, 130
  Access, 147
  data, 97, 101
  importing from the Web, 150–151
  See also databases; lists
task panes, 3–7
templates, 3–4
  creating from workbooks, 14
  spreadsheet, 133
text
  converting to data, 144–146
  correcting automatically, 31
  entering, 17–18
  filtering, on, 141
  See also formatting
Text To Speech, 196–197

textures, 123
time, 17, 22–24, 71
titles
  centering, 43
  chart, 84, 94
  page, 73
  See also headings
toolbars, 10
  adding macros to, 194
  customizing, 8–9
  displaying, 7–8, 10
  restoring defaults on, 9
Total row, 130, 134–135
tracking changes, 171, 173–174
trendlines, 103
trimming. *See* cropping

U

unions, 54
updating
  external references, 59–60, 117, 151–152
  imported data, 152
  shared workbooks, 173–174
  web pages, 181, 182, 183

V

validate data, 136–138
values (Y) axis, 90
views, 174–175

W

web pages,
  creating, 177–193
  importing to Excel, 150
  renaming or relocating, 184
  saving as single files, 184–185
  updating, 183
  using, 183–184
  See also interactive; noninteractive
WordArt, 109, 118–119
workbooks
  closing, 14
  creating new, 4, 5

International Contact Information

AUSTRALIA
McGraw-Hill Book Company Australia Pty. Ltd.
TEL +61-2-9900-1800
FAX +61-2-9878-8881
http://www.mcgraw-hill.com.au
books-it_sydney@mcgraw-hill.com

CANADA
McGraw-Hill Ryerson Ltd.
TEL +905-430-5000
FAX +905-430-5020
http://www.mcgraw-hill.ca

GREECE, MIDDLE EAST, & AFRICA
(Excluding South Africa)
McGraw-Hill Hellas
TEL +30-210-6560-990
TEL +30-210-6560-993
TEL +30-210-6560-994
FAX +30-210-6545-525

MEXICO (Also serving Latin America)
McGraw-Hill Interamericana Editores S.A. de C.V.
TEL +525-1500-5108
FAX +525-117-1589
http://www.mcgraw-hill.com.mx
carlos_ruiz@mcgraw-hill.com

SINGAPORE (Serving Asia)
McGraw-Hill Book Company
TEL +65-6863-1580
FAX +65-6862-3354
http://www.mcgraw-hill.com.sg
mghasia@mcgraw-hill.com

SOUTH AFRICA
McGraw-Hill South Africa
TEL +27-11-622-7512
FAX +27-11-622-9045
robyn_swanepoel@mcgraw-hill.com

SPAIN
McGraw-Hill/Interamericana de España, S.A.U.
TEL +34-91-180-3000
FAX +34-91-372-8513
http://www.mcgraw-hill.es
professional@mcgraw-hill.es

UNITED KINGDOM, NORTHERN,
EASTERN, & CENTRAL EUROPE
McGraw-Hill Education Europe
TEL +44-1-628-502500
FAX +44-1-628-770224
http://www.mcgraw-hill.co.uk
emea_queries@mcgraw-hill.com

ALL OTHER INQUIRIES Contact:
McGraw-Hill/Osborne
TEL +1-510-420-7700
FAX +1-510-420-7703
http://www.osborne.com
omg_international@mcgraw-hill.com